TRAPPERS OF THE WEST

(

TRAPPERS
OF THE WEST

FRED REINFELD

Illustrated by Douglas Gorsline

THOMAS Y. CROWELL COMPANY NEW YORK

BY THE AUTHOR

Commemorative Stamps of the U.S.A.
They Almost Made It
Trappers of the West

The author is most grateful to Thomas Dutelle and
his able staff at the East Meadow Public Library for
their gracious and persevering efforts in tracking down
obscure but invaluable research material for him.

CONTENTS

1 BEYOND THE MISSISSIPPI

BACK IN the seventeenth century the British Crown, in granting charters to groups settling on the Atlantic coast of America, had given them titles to lands stretching to the Pacific. No one knew just where the Pacific was. Perhaps it was two hundred miles inland, perhaps a little farther. No one in those days dreamed that it was three thousand miles away.

In the years that followed, the fog of ignorance lifted, but much still remained to be known. No one knew the exact location and extent of the Rocky Mountains, for example. Some called them "the Shining Mountains," and wove all sorts of fantastic legends about them.

What did white men know about the area beyond the Mississippi? The Spaniards had settled thinly in the Southwest and in California. The French had founded a few straggling posts on the Mississippi. The Hudson's Bay Company had penetrated across the continent into the Northwest.

And that was all. Here was a wilderness occupying millions of square miles—mountains, plains, deserts, rivers. It was occupied—sparsely—by tribes of Indians. Huge herds of buffalo roamed the plains. The rest was legend and ludicrous error.

More than two centuries of exploration had supplied skimpy knowledge, and what little was known had been jealously kept secret so that it would not fall into the hands of rival colonial powers.

In 1528 a Spaniard named Álvar Núñez Cabeza de Vaca was shipwrecked in the Gulf of Mexico. Together with several companions he reached land in the vicinity of present-day Galveston, Texas. For eight years these unfortunate men endured slavery, sickness, and hunger as they wandered through Texas, New Mexico, Arizona, and California, and finally made their way down to Mexico City.

The stories told by the weary travelers aroused the interest of the Viceroy of Mexico. For years the Indians had dazzled the Spaniards with tales of the fabulous riches stored in the Seven Cities of Cíbola. The Viceroy was taken in by these cock-and-bull stories, and in 1539 he assigned Francisco Vásquez de Coronado the command of a force of a thousand men to find the legendary treasures.

Clad in full armor—hardly the appropriate costume for

travel in the Southwest—the Spaniards went diligently on their fool's errand. When they reached the fancied site of the Seven Cities in New Mexico, there was no treasure to reward them. Craftily the Indians led them on from one place to another. The treasure kept receding from them as if it were a desert mirage, and the Indians always got rid of their dangerous guests by telling them that the treasure would turn up "a little farther ahead."

In this way the Spaniards spent two weary years wandering through Arizona, New Mexico, Texas, Colorado, Oklahoma, Kansas—even Nebraska! They were the first white men to see Grand Canyon and the "hunchbacked kine" (buffalo) of the Great Plains. But they found no gold, and that doubtless explains why the Spaniards had no great interest in further exploring the vast domain they had carved out.

More than two centuries passed before they began to colonize California. The Spaniards settled there for a variety of reasons—to convert the Indians to Christianity, to forestall the efforts of the Russians and the British to gain a foothold there, and to found settlements in an area where the climate was agreeable and making a living was easy.

The French fur traders and explorers had been more alert and more enterprising than the Spaniards. In their search for furs, the French had systematically made their way inland, making skillful use of the waterways. First they penetrated down the St. Lawrence, then through the Great Lakes, which brought them to the heart of the continent.

In time they reached the Mississippi Valley and explored the great river all the way down to New Orleans. The work of these daring men culminated one day in 1682 when Robert Cavelier, Sieur de la Salle, having traveled the length of the Mississippi, claimed *the whole drainage basin of the Mississippi and its tributaries* for the French Crown, and named the unknown area "Louisiana" for his King, Louis XIV.

The French had more than a century to explore this area, and they had the men, too. But unfortunately they lacked the necessary funds and backing. French kings were too preoccupied with frittering away human lives and wealth on futile, bloody wars in Europe. And so in time they lost Canada and still continued to ignore the Louisiana Territory.

Even in the face of this foolish policy, the intrepid French fur traders and explorers pressed forward. The most notable expedition was perhaps the one undertaken by the Vérendrye (Louis Joseph and François) brothers in 1742–1743. This expedition apparently got as far west as the Black Hills, for in 1913 a little girl found a marked lead plate near Pierre, South Dakota, which had been buried by the explorers.

Of more direct practical importance were the posts founded by French fur traders at points where the Mississippi was joined by its tributaries. The post destined to play the outstanding role in the fur trade was St. Louis, near the junction point of the Missouri and Mississippi rivers.

The firm of Maxent, Laclede and Company received a monopoly on the Missouri fur trade from the French government in 1762. The following year Pierre Laclede, one of the partners, led an expedition up the Mississippi from New Orleans. Laclede saw the strategic importance of locating a trading post where "the Big Muddy" joins "the Father of Waters," and selected the site of the post.

Laclede named the post St. Louis, in honor of the King's patron saint, and entrusted his associate and second in command, René August Chouteau—then fourteen years old!—with the building of the post. In pioneering times there was always a shortage of people to do needed work. Children and young people were often entrusted with tasks and responsibilities that would be unthinkable in our own day.

From the first, St. Louis became the capital of the fur trade. It took the French traders very little time to recognize the importance of traveling up the Missouri to do business with the Indians by bartering trade goods for their beaver pelts. However, the traders were very timid about ascending the Missouri. How that great river became the classic waterway of the fur trade will be described later on.

April 30, 1803, was a momentous day in American history —perhaps second in importance only to July 4, 1776.

It was on that date that representatives of the United States and France prepared the text of a treaty that enabled the young republic to more than double its territory. By a few pen strokes the United States became a continental power.

What exactly was bought in this famous Louisiana Purchase? No man living on that day knew precisely. The vast area west of the Mississippi was a mystery. It had never been properly mapped; it had not even been fully traversed by white men.

In the years to come the American fur trappers were to become familiar with this mysterious region, and gradually their knowledge was to seep into the consciousness of the people "in the States."

However, with the benefit of hindsight we can see what made up the area west of the Mississippi. Out of the Louisiana Territory were eventually carved all of the states of Missouri, Arkansas, Iowa, Nebraska, and North and South Dakota; also parts of the states of Louisiana, Minnesota, Kansas, Colorado, Montana, Wyoming, and Oklahoma.

At that time a great deal of the region beyond the Mississippi belonged to Spain (later to Mexico). This included all the territory of the future states of Texas, New Mexico, Arizona, California, Nevada, and Utah. Spanish territory also took in parts of Oklahoma, Kansas, Colorado, and Wyoming. All in all, a very considerable area.

But this still does not include all the land west of the Mississippi. Up in the Northwest there was the "Oregon country," which included all of the present-day states of Washington, Oregon, and Idaho, as well as small sections of Montana and Wyoming.

Both the United States and Great Britain laid claim to the "Oregon country." And it was the coming struggle for control of the fur trade that was to lead to the rousing cry of "Fifty-four forty or fight" and bring both countries to the brink of war.

The French government, as we have seen, had always been indifferent to the idea of exploring the Louisiana

Territory. But Thomas Jefferson, who was President at the time of the Louisiana Purchase, was keenly interested in obtaining more information about this huge area. And so he induced Congress to appropriate the substantial sum of $2500 to finance a scientific and exploring expedition.

To assure the success of the expedition into unknown and possibly dangerous country, Jefferson needed a leader who was trustworthy, resourceful, and levelheaded. He found that leader in his young friend and personal secretary, Meriwether Lewis.

To guard against the disastrous possibility that the expedition might fail if Lewis were killed or became seriously ill, a coleader was added: Lewis's close friend William Clark, a younger brother of the famous Revolutionary hero George Rogers Clark. Both men were admirably equipped to do the job that Jefferson wanted—to explore the country between the Mississippi and the Pacific, to map their route, and to keep a journal describing the trip and listing details about the Indian tribes, the plants and animals, and other natural-history features they would find on the way.

Lewis and Clark were both army officers, and the forty-five men they selected with great care were all enlisted into the army in order to place the expedition under military discipline. The party left St. Louis in March, 1804, in a flat-bottomed boat equipped with sail and oars. The leaders intended to ascend the Missouri—not part of the way, but as far as it would take them.

When they set out, they did not know that the Missouri is 2466 miles long—longer than the Mississippi (2348 miles). Nor did they know that the Missouri would present maddening problems of navigation all the way.

Going up the river they passed what are now Missouri, Kansas, Nebraska, Iowa, South Dakota, and North Dakota, and found themselves in Montana. The Missouri continued almost all the way across Montana. In the southwestern corner of what is now Montana, the explorers came to Three Forks, where three rivers came together to form the Missouri. These rivers they named the Jefferson, the Madison, and the Gallatin.

At first Lewis and Clark could not make up their minds

which river to follow. Finally they chose the Jefferson, today known as the Beaverhead. This is the true head-stream of the Missouri, and eventually they came to its ultimate source, a tiny streamlet on the Continental Divide in the Rocky Mountains.

After crossing the Rockies, they still had another thousand miles of difficult travel until they at last caught sight of the Pacific Ocean. Jefferson was particularly interested in this last stage of the trip, because it provided the United States government with valuable information about the disputed Oregon country. The return trip was easier and quicker, and they were back in St. Louis in September, 1806.

It would be impossible to overestimate the importance of this epic exploring trip. From this famous expedition stemmed the whole westward movement of the nineteenth century beyond the Mississippi. Almost forty years were to pass, it is true, before the thin trickle of emigration turned into a mighty torrent.

Before the emigration could proceed on a large scale, many still unknown parts of the Far West had to be explored and described precisely. That was the illustrious task that history assigned to the men we know variously as the fur trappers, traders, beaver-hunters, or mountain men.

It was on the fur trade that the Lewis and Clark expedition had its most powerful impact. Now the traders knew that by ascending the Missouri they could arrive right in the heart of the magnificent beaver country of the Rockies, in present-day Montana and Wyoming.

In the light of this discovery, it is interesting to bear in mind that the heyday of the beaver fur trade is usually given as 1807–1843. For 1807 was the year after Lewis and Clark's return to St. Louis; and 1843 was the year of the first great wave of migration along the Oregon Trail.

To have a good understanding of the kind of life the trappers led, it is necessary to know something about the physical features of the Far West.

The Rocky Mountains, which were the favorite haunts of the trappers, make up the longest and highest mountain chains in North America. As geological time is reckoned, these mountains are comparatively young. Geologists belive that the Rockies were formed about sixty million years ago, toward the end of the Cretaceous Period.

At the outer edges of the Rockies, rolling foothills lead to extensive grassy slopes that make excellent grazing. As the winter snows melt in springtime, greenery gradually appears. In the summertime the atmosphere takes on a peculiar cloudless effect which enhances the beauty of the mountain regions. When autumn comes, the plants and flowers are decked out in brilliant hues.

Rough though they were, the trappers were keenly sensitive to the breathtaking beauty of the Rockies. Even daily hardship and danger could not dull the appeal of the mountains for them.

The timbered areas were often made up of forests of cottonwood trees. These were frequently mentioned in trappers' tales. The cottonwood was useful in many ways. It gave the trappers shelter all year round. It provided logs for huts and fuel for cooking and keeping warm. The bark was a valuable food for horses where there was little grass for grazing. Cottonwood logs were also used for making dugout canoes, and for palisades for forts and trading posts.

An important feature of the Rockies is the Continental Divide (also known as the Great Divide). This is a lofty ridge of mountain summits that separates the westward-flowing streams from the eastward-flowing streams. The Divide does not follow a straight line; instead it meanders in and out for the length of the continent.

As the Rockies extend all the way from northern Alaska to northern New Mexico, they have always been the most formidable barrier to crossing the continent. For that reason, it was of vital importance to find passes through the Rockies.

The most famous of these is South Pass, discovered by the mountain men, probably in the early 1820's. The name "South Pass" is rather misleading, for it is not located in the South and it does not have the usual appearance of a mountain pass.

South Pass is located in southwestern Wyoming, about midway between St. Louis and the Pacific coast. It was used by pioneers on the Oregon Trail. It was called "South" because it is south of the more northerly passes used by Lewis and Clark in crossing the Rockies. Using South Pass made the transcontinental journey shorter and safer.

We usually think of a pass as a narrow gorge through an otherwise impassable mountain range. But South Pass is a broad valley with a gentle slope that reaches an elevation of 7550 feet. Because of this favorable terrain it was possible for the covered wagons of the pioneers to be taken across South Pass.

Before reaching the Rockies, the overland traveler had to cross the Great Plains, the extensive grasslands that cover an area from western Canada down to the Texas Panhandle, and from the foothills of the Rockies (at an elevation of six thousand feet) to the prairies of the Mississippi Valley.

Today the Great Plains form the eastern part of Montana, Wyoming, Colorado, and New Mexico; the northwestern part of Texas; and the western part of the Dakotas, Nebraska, Kansas, and Oklahoma. When the white man settled in this area he turned much of it into wheat-growing land. But before that it was the home of the Comanches, Cheyennes, Arapahoes, and other wandering tribes. The Great Plains were also the chief stamping grounds of the vast herds of buffalo that furnished most of the necessities of existence for the fierce Plains Indians.

The weather on the Plains is often given to extremes. The sun seems to pour down with unusual ferocity, and fierce storms are particularly troublesome for the lonely traveler caught in the open. In *The Oregon Trail*, Francis Parkman gives this wry description of a June day on the plains:

"This very morning was close and sultry, the sun rising with a faint oppressive heat; when suddenly darkness gathered in the west, and a furious burst of sleet and hail drove full in our faces, icy cold, and surged with such demoniac vehemence that it felt like a storm of needles."

If such an oversupply of water was inconvenient, its opposite—total lack of water—could be much more painful. The trapper was often called upon to cross desolate areas without water, and accounts of trapping expeditions give a graphic description of how the men suffered on such trips.

Of the greater trappers, Jed Smith in particular left harrowing accounts of his desert crossings. Part of his graphic description of a journey over the Great Salt Lake Desert is quoted in Chapter Seven. The Mojave Desert of California was another bleak area that the trappers dreaded.

Since overland travel had more than its share of hardship and danger, the trappers tried to make use of waterways wherever they could. The most popular waterway was of course the Missouri River, which brought the trappers to some of the finest beaver country in the West.

But traveling upstream on "the Big Muddy" was always a severe trial of patience. The trappers used keelboats—

broad, flat-bottomed vessels with plenty of room amidships for supplies and trade goods for the Indians. The trappers, by the way, were not idle passengers. They performed some of the hardest work of their lives propelling the keelboats up the Missouri.

When they had a good wind and no obstacles in the stream, they used sail. On the shallow parts of the river they drove the boat ahead by using poles; or else they fastened a rope to some fixed object farther ahead on their course and then wound the other end of the rope around the boat capstan.

The hardest way of all was using the "cordelle," or tow-line. One end of a rope was fastened to the boat, while the other end of the rope was pulled by a group of men on shore. On good days, all their exertions produced a speed of perhaps two miles an hour.

When Francis Parkman traveled up the river, he noted some of the difficulties:

"The Missouri is constantly changing its course, wearing away its banks on one side, while it forms new ones on the other. Its channel is constantly shifting. Islands are formed, and then washed away, and while the old forests on one side are undermined and swept off, a young growth springs up from the new soil on the other. With all these changes, the water is so charged with mud and sand that in spring it is perfectly opaque, and in a few minutes deposits a sediment an inch thick in the bottom of a tumbler."

But this was not all. On its way downstream the turbulent river swept with it an ever greater burden of debris: earth, gravel, boughs, underbrush, logs, bodies of dead animals—all sorts of flotsam.

Sometimes the current was so swift that it forced the keelboat back. There were places where the river was too deep for the poles to touch bottom. Again, there were times when the soil on the banks was too sandy for the men to keep a foothold while towing the boat from shore.

Another danger arose from trees known as "snags." These were rooted in the ooze of the river floor. They projected above the surface of the water, and the force of the current bent them downstream. Other snags were even worse. There were, for example, the "breaks"—logs that were hidden below the surface. There were also the "sawyers," logs that were fastened firmly to their roots below and yet rose and fell with a violence capable of overturning a boat or smashing its bottom. In the worst cases the boatmen had to chop off the snags before they could make progress.

Nor was this all; there were quicksands and sandbars and the dreaded "embarras"—a kind of log jam fastened together by driftwood and other debris. Such an obstacle was wide enough to partly dam up the river, forcing the current to shoot through the free side with a force even greater than usual.

In shallow parts of the river the men might get out and wade through the water dragging the tow rope. Under such conditions, ten miles a day upriver was considered excellent progress. To make matters worse, frequent spring rains soaked the men to the bone, and sent great trees crashing down right on the course.

Sometimes there were winds so powerful that they capsized the broad-beamed keelboat. If the men were lucky no one would be drowned, but all supplies and goods would be lost.

There was still another exasperating feature to the trip. In some parts the channel wound around so crookedly that a three-day voyage of thirty miles left the boat less than a mile away from the original starting point!

Happy indeed were the trappers when the steamboat was introduced on the upper Missouri in 1831. This powerful monster that progressed by belching black smoke made a deep impression on the Indians. They considered it notable "medicine"—a strong proof of the white man's magical powers.

One of the consequences of the growth of civilization has been the steady decline in the number of wild animals. Thousands of years ago primitive man had to be ever watchful to defend himself against formidable beasts. As recently as 1800 the North American continent was a paradise for wild life. Today this is no longer so true, especially as regards the more dangerous or more valuable animals.

Think of the buffalo, for example, which once roamed as far east as northern Florida, central Georgia, and western Pennsylvania. It ranged as far north as Great Slave Lake, about eight hundred miles north of the Canadian border. It could be found as far south as Texas, as far west as Oregon.

In Daniel Boone's time so many buffalo made their ponderous way to the Blue Licks of Kentucky for salt that he described the buffalo trails leading there as "like the streets of a great city." Yet by 1820 not a single buffalo could be found east of the Mississippi.

At that time there were perhaps 60,000,000 buffalo on the Great Plains. Today there are about five thousand left in the United States. The coming of the white man to the West resulted in the mass slaughter of these animals.

To the Indians—and the trappers, too—buffalo meat was the tastiest and most nourishing of all foods. In addition to food, the carcass of the buffalo provided shelter, weapons, and many other things.

The grizzly bear, on the other hand, was a dangerous

enemy. This "beast that walks like a man" measures about six feet from nose to tail tip, but lengths of nine to fourteen feet have been observed. It weighs from six hundred to one thousand pounds.

As a rule the grizzly is cautious and timid, but when aroused it is transformed into a fierce, tenacious battler. A powerful blow from one of its formidable forepaws can be fatal. In addition, its sharp claws and gouging and rending teeth can inflict deadly wounds. Luckily for its potential victims, somewhere between the ages of one and two years the grizzly loses the curvature of its claws, so that it cannot climb trees.

Though there are now only about six hundred grizzlies in the United States, they were once quite common, especially in the West. One trapper reported seeing over two hundred in a single day, while another trapper mentions killing five grizzlies in twenty-four hours. Even after making allowances for the frontier habit of concocting tall tales, the number of grizzlies must have been considerable.

Tales of trapper life are full of stories about narrow escapes from these huge, tough, dangerous animals. A frontiersman who had an encounter with "Old Ephraim," as they nicknamed the grizzly, had something to talk about for the rest of his days. Daniel Boone once inscribed on a tree this legend: "D. Boone kilt a bar hear." Jed Smith and Kit Carson had notable grizzly encounters, which are described later on in this book.

But even mountain men who faced "Old Ephraim" un-afraid could be terrified by rattlesnakes. What nightmare could be worse than dreaming that a rattlesnake had crawled into the trapper's outdoor bed? In the days before the West was settled, these creatures were quite numerous. They might be seen at times in groups of hundreds, sunning them-selves on bare rock.

The rattlesnake has two fangs through which it gives off its poison. Its most terrifying characteristic is the rattle by which it announces its presence. Yet it is not aggressive, attacking only when it is taken by surprise.

Despite the horror that mankind has always had for snakes, both Indians and mountain men occasionally ate snake flesh when goaded by hunger pangs. In fact, some trappers claimed that snake meat was an exceptional deli-cacy. The Indians used the skin, teeth, and rattles of these snakes for ornament, doubtless to give themselves a for-midable appearance and also to take on the powers of the dead animals. It was one of the Indian's most cherished magical beliefs that with the proper incantations he could assume the qualities of the creatures he had killed.

This, then, was the world in which the mountain man lived. We come now to the most important element of that world—the Indians who had dwelt there for thousands of years before the coming of the white man.

2 THE DISINHERITED

DURING THE 1820's and 1830's there were never more than about a thousand trappers in the West. Yet these few men were the advance scouts for the later emigration of thousands upon thousands of pioneers that acquired momentum in the 1840's. Thus, without quite realizing it, the mountain men played a decisive role in the relentless struggle between the white man and the Indian that had started with the discovery of the New World.

It was an unequal struggle from the start. The Indians were bound to be overwhelmed by sheer force of numbers. At the beginning of the nineteenth century, there were perhaps half a million Indians living west of the Mississippi. Some of the most famous tribes, notable for their implacable enmity to the white man, could hardly have numbered more than ten thousand—and quite possibly considerably

21

less. And this figure included not only able-bodied warriors, but also women, children, and the aged.

Nor was this all. Living conditions for the pioneers were crude and primitive, to be sure, but they were incomparably superior to those that prevailed among the Indians. In 1800 the Indians were still living as in the Late Stone Age, thousands of years behind their white rivals. Stone axes and flint arrowheads could hardly combat rifles and cannon.

For several decades the dismal truth went unrealized by the Indians. As long as the West was thinly populated by a handful of mountain men, the danger of being overwhelmed seemed remote indeed. In fact, the mountain men, thousands of miles away from civilization, lived more like Indians than like the white men of town and farm. As long as small numbers of white trappers wandered in the wilderness in their quest for beaver pelts, the Indians continued to lord it over the West. Once the white men thronged to the West to live in settled communities, the odds were hopelessly against the Indians.

It is difficult to understand the Indian's plight because for centuries there has been a good deal of romanticizing about the way he lived. People who are ruled by schedule and routine and tied to humdrum tasks are bound to look longingly to the Indian's pleasant outdoor life, his freedom from monotonous work and responsibility.

The Indian had long ago decided that work was degrading for a male. He solved the problem by saddling his squaw with all the drudgery that is incidental to living. When the Indian brave was not occupied with killing and hunting, he spent his days lazily, playing gambling games with the other men or swapping stories.

On a busy city street the Indian might have appeared ludicrous, but on his home grounds he was an impressive figure. Francis Parkman felt this as he described an Indian he met on the Great Plains:

"His head was shaved and painted red, and from the tuft of hair remaining on the crown dangled several eagle's feathers and the tails of two or three rattlesnakes. His cheeks, too, were daubed with vermillion; his ears were adorned with green glass pendants; a collar of grizzly bears' claws surrounded his neck, and several large necklaces hung on his breast."

But closer acquaintance with Indian life made it seem much less attractive. The Indian lacked many of the simplest creature comforts. He was exposed to bad weather to an extent that most white men would have found intolerable. The Plains Indian never had a settled home; he was always on the move, always wandering. His temporary villages were squalid and noisy.

The din of an Indian village was proverbial. One traveler of the 1840's speaks of the Indians' "obstreperous mirth, their whooping and howling and quarreling . . . yelling like fiends, the barking and baying of savage wolf-dogs, and the incessant cracking of rifles."

As long as the Indian was able to follow the trail of the buffalo, he was freed from the danger of periodic famine. But where food was scarce, the Indian had a hard time of it. The Digger Indians of California, for example, developed what seems to us a strange and repulsive diet for lack of an adequate food supply.

These Indians lived mostly on ants and grasshoppers. They would gather ants in large quantities, wash off the dirt, and pound them into a "pastry" which was considered an epicure's delight. Some of these Indians, we are told, ate live ants by the handful.

Father de Smet, a famous Jesuit missionary who lived among the Digger Indians of California, explained that they got their name from the practice of digging holes in the ground about five feet deep with a diameter of ten or twelve feet and then driving all the nearby grasshoppers into the hole.

"They have their tastes like other people," he wrote. "Some eat the grasshoppers in soup; others mash them and make a kind of pie of them, which they harden or bake in the sun or dry by a fire; others still take pointed sticks, on which they string the larger grasshoppers, and as fast as they are sufficiently roasted the poor Indians regale themselves until the repast is entirely consumed."

Many Indian tribes were seemingly callous to their older folk, especially in the wintertime when food was short and there was not enough to go around. This is well brought out in Frémont's description of a pathetic incident that took place during his third expedition.

It was nighttime. Frémont's men, weary from a hard day's travel, were stretched out comfortably near the campfire. Suddenly Kit Carson exclaimed excitedly: "Good God! Look there!"

In the light of the fire they saw a very aged woman who looked eighty if not more, with disheveled gray hair hanging down over her face and shoulders. She shielded her eyes from the blaze with her gnarled, emaciated hands. She had blundered toward the camp, thinking she would find Indians were there. When she saw that the men were whites, she gasped with terror. She tried to escape, but the men escorted her gently to the warmth of the fire.

Then "she made us understand that she had been left by her people to die, because she was very old and was no longer good for anything. She told us she had nothing to eat and was very hungry." The men gave her some food, but instead of sitting down to eat it, she scampered off.

When the Indian was sick or wounded, his chances of recovery depended—so he thought, with his Stone Age mentality—on ritual chants and dances, as well as ointments that were thought to have a magical effect. The medicine man provided good-luck charms and spells—this in an age when medical research was making giant strides. Here we see one of the many ways in which the unfortunate Indians were hopelessly handicapped in their life-and-death struggle with the whites.

Despite their general appearance of great physical strength, the Indians succumbed with pitiable swiftness to the diseases of the white man. As they had not been previously subject to these ailments, their bodies had built up no resistance to them.

The worst instance of this was the terrible smallpox epidemic of 1837, which was transmitted up the Missouri by a trappers' expedition containing equipment that included four infected blankets. With lightning speed the dread disease spread from one tribe to another. Many a tribe lost half its people.

In the case of the Mandans, a South Dakota tribe, only 10 per cent escaped death; the survivors had to go to live with neighboring tribes. This tragedy had its ironic side, for the Mandans had a perfect record of unbroken friendship for the white man, going back even further than the first visit of Lewis and Clark to their villages.

Still, there were times when the Indians displayed great skill in treating diseases with which they were familiar. A notable instance of this occurred in 1845, when William Bent, the leading trader of the Southwest, fell ill with a disease that to modern doctors sounds like diphtheria. A famous Cheyenne medicine man was brought to examine the sick man. He depressed Bent's tongue with a spoon handle and scrutinized his throat. Seeing that it was infected, the Indian decided to extract the pus.

Going outside the tepee, the medicine man gathered some sandburs with sharp thorns. With a bone awl he made a small hole in each of the burs and then strung them all on a sinew thread. After tying the burs to a notched stick, he smeared them with marrow fat and then inserted the stick in the sick man's throat. As he pulled up the burs, the infected matter came along with them.

Soon the patient felt much better. The pain in his throat was relieved, and he was able to swallow soup. He improved rapidly and the infection was soon cured. Without the medicine man's treatment he would probably have died.

The Plains Indian had two great interests—killing tribal enemies and stealing horses. Killing was always followed by scalping and often by horrible mutilations of the dead body. These traits were stark expressions of the Indian's fierce warlike attitude. Francis Parkman observed that "the man is encased in an impenetrable exterior—within he may be full of hatred, malice, and suspicion, but none of this appears. He is a statue." Yet "he lives in constant fear. The world to him is full of spirits."

An army officer who was in daily contact with the Plains Indians for over thirty years, and later wrote a book about them, characterized them in these words:

"Cruelty is both an amusement and a study. So much pleasure is derived from it, that an Indian is constantly thinking out new devices of torture, and how to prolong to the utmost those already known."

Because of the Indian's preoccupation with torture, he taught his children that the highest virtue of an Indian brave was to endure pain without the slightest sign of suffering; the greatest proof of manliness was to taunt one's tormentors. It is almost impossible to explain such an attitude, or to account for a deed like this one related by a boastful Sioux warrior.

One night he stealthily approached a Pawnee village a thousand miles away from his own home. Sneaking into a tepee, "he unsheathed his knife and, stirring the fire, coolly selected his victims. One by one he stabbed and scalped them, when a child suddenly awoke and screamed. He rushed from the lodge, yelled a Sioux war cry, shouted his name in triumph and defiance, and darted out upon the black prairie, leaving the whole village in a tumult with the howling and baying of dogs, the screams of women, and the yells of enraged warriors."

All the Indian tribes had the custom of "counting coups" —public boasting by warriors in which they described their achievements as fighting men. Brandishing the scalps of their victims was the best evidence that their boasts were grim truth. The institution of "counting coups" stimulated each brave to the appropriate pitch of bloodthirstiness, since it was an appeal to his pride.

To the Indian a scalp was a scalp, whether it had come from a well-armed enemy or a defenseless woman. Such thinking was understandable in a savage, but it was less excusable in the whites, who had been brought up in the gentling tradition of a noble religion.

In the matter of scalping, the whites were by no means blameless. Many trappers took scalps in their fights with Indians and proudly dangled these trophies at their belts. Actually, the custom of scalping by whites goes back quite far in our history. Not only the colonies, but later on the state governments offered bounties for scalps of Indians.

Take the case of Hannah Dunstin, a matron of Haverhill, Massachusetts. In 1697 she was carried off with a young boy in an Indian raid. Several nights later Mrs. Dunstin killed nine of her captors, and the boy killed another Indian. Before fleeing, Mrs. Dunstin scalped all ten men in order to have evidence of her exploit. When she returned home, she displayed the scalps to a colonial court, which awarded her £25 for loss of property.

Brutal Indian raids often brought even more brutal retaliation by white men. There were times when vengeful punishment by the whites was out of all proportion to the original crime.

For example, when a band of the treacherous Arikaras of South Dakota stole some horses from a group of mountain men, the trappers captured two of the thieving Indians. The rest of the Arikaras offered to swap two stolen animals for the captives, but the trappers insisted on the return of all the animals. At this the Indians shrugged and departed, leaving their unfortunate comrades to their fate. Infuriated because they were deprived of their mounts, the trappers burned their prisoners to death.

So the unequal struggle went on, with the Indians eventually greatly outnumbered and at a severe disadvantage. Though they fought back with all the traditional bravery, fighting skill, and fortitude of their race, they were relentlessly driven from their lands and their sources of food.

3 THE BEAVER TRADE AND THE STRUGGLE FOR EMPIRE

THE USE of furs as both a necessity and a luxury goes back to prehistoric times. Primitive man, huddled in the murky gloom of a cave, tried to keep himself warm by wearing furs. Even today the lack of efficient heating still makes furs a necessity for indoor wear in many parts of the world.

But furs have also been, and still are, a means of display —a symbol of aristocracy and wealth. During the Middle Ages, for example, the handsomest furs were worn by kings, nobility, and the higher clergy. In those days, and later too, "sumptuary" laws were passed or decreed to forbid the wearing of the finest furs by people who did not belong to one of the privileged groups.

Early in the seventeenth century beaver hats became the fashion in Europe. As a matter of fact the so-called beaver hat was mostly of rabbit felt, with a beaver fur surface. Though fashion is notoriously fickle, this was one style that had a long life—somewhat longer than two centuries. About 1800, when the vogue was approaching its end, it was revived because Beau Brummell, the famous English dandy, was very partial to the beaver hat.

The next three decades or so were the Golden Age of the beaver trade. Then several things happened. Intensive trapping along the beaver streams of the American Far West left the animals in short supply. Hatmakers knew they would have to be seeking a substitute material.

And such substitutes were available. There was seal, supplied by the Russians in great quantity; there was nutria from South America. But above all the China trade, rising to considerable proportions, introduced silk as the fashionable material for hats.

As early as 1833, John Jacob Astor, who had made a fortune in furs, wrote to a business associate: "I very much fear beaver will not sell well very soon unless very fine. It appears that they make hats out of silk in place of beaver." And so, as the silk hat increased in popularity, the price of beaver pelts fell disastrously. It no longer paid to trap beaver. The beaver hat was ready to take its place in the museums.

The fur trade was the first large-scale business enterprise in North America, and up to the end of the eighteenth century it was the most important; so much so that Great Britain and France fought three wars in the New World during the 1700's for the mastery of the fur trade.

It was the French, back in the beginning of the seventeenth century, who first realized how profitable the fur trade could be. As we have seen on page 4, the French made magnificent use of inland waterways to build up their trade in furs. Trade led to exploring, and exploring in turn led to more trade. In time the quest for furs was to sweep right across to the Pacific.

Before the loss of New France to the British in 1763, the French fur traders had built a far-flung series of forts —west to the Canadian Rockies, south to the Arkansas River. Their mighty empire extended from the Arctic Circle to New Orleans, from the mouth of the St. Lawrence to Saskatchewan.

For a long time the French royal monopoly held the fur trade in its secure grip. In order to dispose of their peltries, traders had to pay a heavy tax to the government at the time of sale. On top of that, officials of New France extorted heavy sums before granting them a license to sell.

Among the ablest and most daring traders of the day were Pierre Radisson and his brother-in-law Médard Chouart, Sieur des Groseilliers. On a pioneering trip north, they discovered that the Hudson Bay wilderness was incalculably rich in fur-bearing animals. Returning with several hundred thousand dollars' worth of pelts, the two traders were no match for the wily and grasping officials of New France. Radisson and Groseilliers were mulcted so shamelessly that they ended up with only one-fifth the value of their furs.

Understandably infuriated, the two men sailed to England in order to reveal the secret of untold wealth to the English. Their story created a sensation. Not only the reigning king, Charles II, but many noblemen and wealthy merchants as well, were enthralled by the vista of fabulous riches. They struggled with Groseilliers' name—the nearest they got to it was "Mr. Gooseberry"—but they had no trouble comprehending the value of the fur trade.

And so in 1670 Charles II granted a fantastically sweeping charter to "the Governor and Company of Adventurers trading into Hudson's Bay." (Although Hudson Bay is in Canada, then a French colony, the British claimed the region on the basis of Henry Hudson's explorations there on his last voyage in 1610. This claim was one that the French accepted grudgingly in peacetime, and disputed actively in wartime.)

As was the fashion in those days, the royal charter gave the Hudson's Bay Company title to all the rivers that empty into the bay and all the land drained by those rivers. While no one knew it then, this gave the company almost a million and a half square miles. In return, all that the Crown asked for was that whenever a British monarch entered the company's territory, he was to be presented with "two Black Beavers." This provision was scrupulously kept during the royal visits to Canada in the twentieth century.

From the very start the Company's business was extremely profitable. After building and manning several forts, it outfitted three ships which made an annual voyage to the New World, bringing supplies west and taking furs east.

Low overhead was the key to the Company's operations. The fur-bearing animals raised their pelts in the wilderness at their own expense, so to speak; the Company did not have to feed and maintain them. Then the Indians trapped the animals—still at no expense to the Company—and brought the pelts to the Company post. There the pelts were turned in for trade goods at a profit of 600 per cent—often more—to the Company.

The French operated in a different fashion. Their colonists loved the mysterious forests and the well-stocked streams. They were skilled "woods-runners" (*coureurs de bois*) and superb canoemen (*voyageurs*). The ways of the Indians

appealed to them; they generally married Indian girls; the staid life of the farmer was not for them.

After a while, as rivalry became keen, the British had to copy the French system of going to the Indians for the pelts. Each side invaded the other's territory. There were hot disputes and bloodshed too, for a great empire was at stake. The legality of the British claim might enchant lawyers, but it was ordained that the mastery of the North American fur trade would have to be decided by brute force.

Even the British triumph of 1763 at the end of the French and Indian War, which gave them Canada, did not close the question of competition. For now individual traders —"free traders" as they were called—began to push west. After several unsuccessful attempts, some of these traders and a group of Montreal merchants organized the North West Company as a competitor to the Hudson's Bay Company.

The North West Company brought the old French system to its highest point of efficiency. Operating over thousands of miles of inland waterways, it sent its skilled *voyageurs* in swift thirty-two-foot canoes that carried trade goods to the Indians and brought back pelts. Though the canoes were light enough to be carried on portages for miles, they were also sturdy enough to hold a four-ton cargo.

The competition between the two companies was pitiless. Killing, plundering, and small-scale war became commonplace in the struggle. But they had constructive achievements to their credit too. For example, Alexander Mackenzie of the North West Company was the first white man to cross the Rockies (in Canada) and to reach the Pacific by land. He accomplished both these feats in 1793.

David Thompson, another employee of the North West Company, devoted a large part of his life to exploring the West. He was the first man to make a careful study of the basin of the Columbia River and its tributaries in Washington, British Columbia, Idaho, and Montana.

Thompson had a knack of graphic description which a friend portrayed in these words: "He has a very powerful mind and a singular faculty of picture-making. He can create a wilderness and people it with warring savages, or climb the Rocky Mountains with you in a snowstorm, so clearly and palpably, that only shut your eyes and you hear the crack of the rifle, or feel the snow flakes melt on your cheeks as he talks."

By 1803, the year of the Louisiana Purchase, the fur trade in the Oregon country had reached a fiercely competitive state. In those days, as you will recall from page 7, the "Oregon" region was made up of present-day Washington, Oregon, and Idaho, plus small sections of Montana and Wyoming.

The Hudson's Bay Company traders and the North West Company men were at each other's throats. At the same time the British government claimed the whole vast

"Oregon" country. Consequently it had a strong interest in seeing peace prevail between the Canadian posts in the Oregon country.

Meanwhile the United States was also claiming the Oregon country. By the beginning of the nineteenth century American traders hailing from Boston were delivering fourteen thousand pelts to China—a business that amounted to almost half a million dollars a year.

These traders used a profitable "triangular-voyage" method in doing business with China. Their vessels started out from Boston with a cargo of supplies and trade goods. Rounding Cape Horn, the ships sailed to the mouth of the Columbia River. There the traders loaded pelts on the vessels and sent them off to China, where the furs were sold. Picking up merchandise in the Orient, they returned to New England with a new cargo that brought them handsome profits.

Average-grade beaver skins were disposed of to the hatmakers. The best beaver skins were kept for the China trade or for furriers who made coats from them. Sea otter, the most valuable fur of all, was a specialty of the Russian traders who had established themselves in Alaska during the eighteenth century.

It was a complicated situation, which became even more complicated when John Jacob Astor decided to join the fun. Astor was born in 1763 in Waldorf, a little German village near Heidelberg. As a youngster he worked for a while in his father's butcher shop. But this hardly suited a young man of Astor's brilliant, restless temperament.

Running away to London, he managed to save enough money to sail to Baltimore four years later. In a few years he became a wealthy man by buying furs in New York and selling them in Europe. By 1808 he was a millionaire.

Astor's ambition was nothing less than to gain control of the whole North American fur trade. To do this he formed the Pacific Fur Company. His first step was to purchase and outfit a ship called the *Tonquin*. Copying the American traders already established on the scene, Astor intended to send the *Tonquin* around the Horn to the mouth of the Columbia River and found a trading post there.

At this ideal location his men could buy sea-otter skins from the coast as well as beaver skins from the hinterland. Astor knew that the Russians were planning a string of trading posts along the Pacific coast, with a view to eventually taking over San Francisco. So he had to compete not only with the Canadian companies but with the Russians as well.

To make success doubly sure, Astor planned to construct a series of forts extending to Oregon from the Great Lakes and from St. Louis. Once he accomplished this, he would have communications with the Oregon country by land and sea, and would be reasonably sure of beating out his rivals.

But the plan was too grandiose. For the time being,

Astor contented himself with equipping an expedition that was to reach the mouth of the Columbia from St. Louis. (Lewis and Clark had shown the way!) This last detail was important. Astor wanted to best the Canadians and the Russians; but at the same time he wanted to have a head start on the other American trappers who would soon be crossing the Rockies into the Oregon country.

Astor's planning was superb. Unfortunately his timing was poor, and his selection of men was even worse. Since he needed men experienced in the fur trade, he got them by hiring them away from the North West Company. This seemed a logical step, but it was foolish. The year was 1810; bitter feeling between the United States and Great Britain was running high. In case of conflict between the two, Astor's Canadians would be torn between two loyalties.

The *Tonquin,* a vessel of 290 tons, with ten guns and a crew of twenty-one, left New York in September, 1810, and arrived at the mouth of the Columbia River the following April. About twelve miles up the river, Astor's men built a fort they called Astoria. To their dismay, the small group left at Astoria soon learned that the whole crew of the *Tonquin* had been killed by Indians who resented the captain's high-handed treatment.

The Astor men who made the grueling overland trip to Oregon also fared badly. The time for their trip was ill chosen, and they had to wait until March, 1811, before they could set out from St. Louis. Constantly they were exposed to attack by the Indians. Before they had covered the two thousand miles to Astoria, they endured every privation of wilderness travel, losing half the members of the expedition on the way.

Messengers assigned to get news back to Astor took nine months to reach St. Louis. The outbreak of the War of 1812 filled him with anxiety, for he realized that his expeditions would be at the mercy of the North West Company men. His fears were well grounded, for his men eventually surrendered Astoria to the North West Company force. Astor had to admit complete failure.

The Oregon boundary dispute continued to simmer. In 1818 American and British diplomats met in a futile attempt to settle the question. The English wanted the border between the United States and Canada to run west from the Lake of the Woods (northern Minnesota) at forty-nine degrees of latitude up to the point where the Columbia River crosses that parallel. Then, said the British, they wanted all of present-day Washington that lies north and west of the Columbia's course to the sea.

This would have amounted to the best two-thirds of Washington. Naturally the Americans were unwilling to part with this huge chunk, and the negotiations reached a stalemate. They did agree, however, that nationals of both sides could come freely to the disputed area.

As matters stood, this region, noted for its magnificent furs, was likely to go to the country that sent in the largest number of trappers. Though the Hudson's Bay and North West Company people had the advantage of being on the spot, the Americans had the advantage for the future. They had a larger population and a nearer base (St. Louis), whereas their Canadian rivals had to work from Montreal.

The British had already reconciled themselves to losing that part of the Oregon country that lay east and south of the Columbia. The best they could hope for was to trap so intensively in this area that by the time they had to get out it would have been turned into a "fur desert."

Thus the trade rivalry between the American and Canadian fur companies and the political rivalry between their countries were so tangled that the two elements could not be separated. What happened eventually was that the efforts of American companies to get their fair share of "Oregon" fur enabled the United States government to get all of modern Washington.

The British government realized that the fierce struggle between the Hudson's Bay Company and the North West Company (as described on page 37) was suicidal. It therefore brought pressure to bear on the younger company to sell out to its rival. The sale took place in 1821, and the unofficial "civil war" came to an end.

Fully aware that the coming struggle for the Oregon country would require the efforts of its best men, the Hudson's Bay Company appointed John McLoughlin to take charge of its posts in that region. McLoughlin, broad-shouldered and well over six feet in height, was thirty-eight at this time, and a man of imposing dignity, kindliness, and distinction. His bearing particularly impressed the Indians, who called him "White Eagle" because of his streak of white hair.

A leader in the fur country had to be a general, a diplomat, a linguist, a doctor, a first-class trapper, and a trader. As a man of outstanding ability, McLoughlin was all these things, and more—he was also a man of culture. He continued to practice his profession of medicine, and books were his greatest delight. Far from living in isolation in the wilderness, he often had the opportunity to entertain scientists and other distinguished visitors.

It was said of McLoughlin's hard-bitten crew that they "kept the Sabbath—and everything else." This was a trade rival's unwilling compliment for McLoughlin's staff. His crew were mostly Scots, intelligent, born to command; men of great capabilities and iron will and endurance. Many of them were well educated, and some of them were graduates of Oxford or the University of Edinburgh.

Three years after his arrival, McLoughlin established his headquarters at Fort Vancouver, sixty miles up the Columbia River. The fort was in the shape of a stockaded rectangle, 750 by 500 feet. The stockade, 20 feet high, provided ample protection against Indian attack.

McLoughlin was too wise to remain dependent on the

East for the post's food supply. Eventually he had fifteen hundred acres under cultivation, as well as a thousand head of cattle. In addition, he encouraged old trappers and hunters to retire and start farms near the fort. Thus these people lived out their lives in a useful and pleasant way, while at the same time the settlement benefited by McLoughlin's wise policy.

There was bitter competition between the Hudson's Bay men and the American fur traders. In dealing with the Indians for pelts, the white men fiercely outbid each other. They encouraged the Indians to steal fur traps from their competitors. Though the Americans used rum as an inducement to get the Indians' furs, McLoughlin frowned on this tactic.

Sometimes, reduced to the last stage of desperation, stray Americans came in a pitiable state to Fort Vancouver. And although the Americans were his ruthless rivals, McLoughlin welcomed them and took good care of them. At the same time he treated the Indians justly and made it his fixed policy to protect them from ill treatment by white men.

With the disappearance of the North West Company, competition had disappeared at the Canadian end of the fur trade. Among the Americans, John Jacob Astor hoped to obtain a similar position, but he never managed to eliminate the other fur-trading outfits.

As we have seen, individual traders did business with the Indians even before the days of Lewis and Clark. Outstanding among the traders around 1800 was Manuel Lisa, a Spaniard who lived in St. Louis. In 1808, after the return of Lewis and Clark, Lisa founded the Missouri Fur Company and ran it until his death in 1820.

Astor was apparently determined to make up for his Oregon fiasco, for he bought out the Missouri Fur Company and entered the upper Missouri Valley trade in 1822.

In that same year the Rocky Mountain Fur Company was started by Andrew Henry and William Henry Ashley. In twelve years this firm handled furs to the value of $500,000. During that time its losses in goods and supplies amounted to $100,000, and seventy of its trappers were killed.

While Astor had much more capital than Henry and Ashley, they had the finest trappers, explorers, and Indian fighters—such men as Jim Bridger, Jed Smith, Kit Carson, and Tom Fitzpatrick.

All the American companies were based on St. Louis, which has remained to this day the capital of the American fur trade. Lewis and Clark had started their expedition from St. Louis, and for years trapping and military expeditions were to follow their example.

In the 1820's, St. Louis was a sprawling town, muddy and dusty by turns, with a population of four or five thousand. Its hotels were of poor quality, there was no night lighting, there were frequent street brawls, and political campaigns were impassioned and noisy.

Much of the town's population was transient—trappers, boatmen, guides, Indians. In fact, visiting Indians set up their tepees in empty lots. On the streets one heard not only English but French and Spanish as well, plus a variety of accents and dialects and Indian tongues.

The steamboat had arrived several years earlier, starting at Pittsburgh and going down the Ohio River and up the Mississippi to St. Louis. Thus St. Louis became the hub for shipping of manufactured goods from the East, crops from the Midwest, cotton from the South, and furs from the Far West.

The fur companies had three different ways of operating. They traded with the Indians for their pelts; they sent their trappers—hired employees—to obtain the furs and bring them back; or else they secured pelts from "free" trappers who were in business for themselves.

Whether a man chose the first, second, or third alternative depended on his abilities and temperament. The most enterprising and self-reliant naturally preferred to strike out on their own. All the famous mountain men—the ones whose names have come down to us—either became "free" trappers or else headed trappers' brigades.

The man in charge of a group of trappers was known as a *bourgeois*—a term handed down from the old days of the French colonial fur trade. (The trappers called him a "booshway.")

The *bourgeois* was assisted by a *commis* (another French

term), a clerk who might some day rise to the master's position. In addition to his clerical work, the *commis* was sometimes in charge of lesser posts, or else he went on trips for the *bourgeois* to Indian villages. If he was good at his work, he had a very promising future.

Voyageurs or *engagés* (also French terms) signed up for three-year engagements with the *bourgeois* at such tasks as paddling cargoes of furs, obtaining food by hunting and fishing, cooking, and so on. Back at the trading post they packed furs and cut timber for firewood. Most of them were French Canadians. They lived very much like Indians, acquired the savages' wilderness skills, and married Indian girls.

After serving a term they were known as *hivernants*—men who had served at least one winter in the wilds. On portages around dangerous rapids the *engagés* would carry the cargo on land. Burdens of as much as 240 pounds were not unknown. Their squaws carried burdens almost as heavy, plus an infant.

The *engagés* were poorly paid—perhaps a hundred dollars and a scanty outfit of two shirts, cowhide boots, and a blanket, for a year's work. Yet, despite their hard work and poor pay, these men enjoyed their lot. Like their French Canadian ancestors, they loved to sing sentimental songs as they paddled along the wilderness streams.

"Hired" trappers worked for regular wages, with traps, weapons, and horses supplied by the fur company. In addition to trapping they also hunted, loaded and unloaded pack animals, and performed any other drudgery that came their way.

The "free" trappers came and went as they pleased. They provided their own animals and equipment, and disposed of their peltries to the highest bidder. In territory infested by Indians, they sometimes attached themselves to a trapping brigade. In return they undertook to trade all their furs to the *bourgeois* or else pay him for the protection they had enjoyed.

Dealing with "free" trappers meant that the company

had to pay more for the pelts it obtained. On the other hand, the company did not have to outfit the men, and the higher pay stimulated the "free" trappers to increase their catch. In actual practice they were the ones who took the greatest risks, and often had little enough to show for their daring.

Much of the fur trade depended on honesty and good faith. When the *bourgeois* sent his trusted clerk to trade with the Indians, he had to place in his charge thousands of dollars' worth of valuable trade goods—blankets, lead for bullets, tobacco, cloth, implements, ornaments, and the like. Again, when the white men gave the Indians credit, they had to wait until the following season to get the Indians' furs to pay off the debt.

The trading situation in the West was somewhat different from what it had been in the Midwest. In Canada and in Michigan, Illinois, Wisconsin, and Minnesota, the Indians needed the white man's weapons and utensils. Consequently they were eager to trap animals and trade pelts to the white man.

But on the Plains and in the foothills of the Rockies, the Indians relied on the buffalo for their food, shelter, clothing, fuel, and many implements. Therefore they were on the whole less in need of articles from the white man and more disposed to fight him.

Besides, stealing the white man's horses was in a way even more profitable than obtaining his wares. Hence the American organizations that started in the fur business after the return of Lewis and Clark had to send their own employees to do the trapping and bring back a large proportion of the furs.

But this did not quite solve the problem, for the hostility of the Indians cut drastically into the profits that could be made in the fur trade. We think of the Indians as the most adventurous element of the Wild West, but from the businessman's point of view they were the chief cause of expense.

In the days when there were about a thousand trappers in the West, the Indians killed one every ten days on the average. This increased the number of men who had to be employed for trapping. The Indians stole horses and supplies, raising the cost of transporting merchandise and of maintaining trading posts.

Much of the trappers' time was spent fighting the Indians, hiding from them, guarding against sudden attack, or chasing them to recover stolen horses. Indian hostility enormously decreased the amount paid to trappers for furs at the annual rendezvous in the Rockies. For the pelts still had to be transported from the Rockies, and who wanted to pay a high price in view of the dangers that would be incurred on the way home through Indian territory?

The most hostile Indians of all were the Blackfeet, who roamed over some of the best fur country of present-day northern Wyoming, Montana, and southern Canada. The

Blackfeet were grand fighters and proud of it. They hated the white man and all his works.

Unlike other tribes, the Blackfeet could not be bought off with liquor or glass beads or even sincere offers of friendship. They were determined to keep their beaver streams for themselves. They meant to kill every white man on sight.

The whites were far from blameless in their dealings with Indians. When Indians arrived at a trading post with their furs, they were often plied with bad liquor and sometimes even drugged. The traders who had no scruples about treating them this way were equally unscrupulous in the actual trading.

Joe Meek, one of the most famous of the mountain men, said of these occasions that "every form of drunkenness, from the simple stupid, the silly, the heroic, the insane, the beastly, the murderous, displayed itself."

In 1844, in one such transaction during the dead of winter in Montana, an Indian tribe "traded" away 210 warm buffalo robes for five gallons of liquor. According to the then current scale of values, a single robe would have been more than enough to pay for all the liquor!

In the fur country there was no police force, no judicial system, no lawmaking body, no government as we understand it. It was American territory for the most part, but there was no one on hand to enforce the law. Many a trapper was a law unto himself. If arguments got too fierce they were settled by gun and dagger. Under these conditions, the *bourgeois* in charge of a trading post had to be a man of firm character and natural authority.

Trading posts were usually built at a spot where a great deal of traffic might be expected, and consequently they were located for the convenience of the Indian tribes. Not one of these forts was ever successfully besieged by hostile Indians.

The walls of the fort were made of thick logs reinforced by crossbeams. These walls formed a stockade, perhaps two hundred feet square, and at two diagonal corners there were blockhouses pierced with loopholes for shooting. Here weapons were stored. The average blockhouse was twelve feet square and twenty feet high.

Also inside the stockade, for protection against the Indians, were the living quarters, as well as carpentry and blacksmith shops, stores, and trading quarters.

Farther south, some forts were built of adobe. This was true of Bent's Fort, in southeastern Colorado. This famous post had walls four feet thick. In addition to loopholes for muskets, its blockhouses had portholes for cannon. The gate was topped by a watchtower manned by members of the garrison. Here they kept watch with a "spyglass" which had a seven-mile range in clear weather.

Bent's Fort had a special council room for conferences with Indians, as well as a common dining hall for the inhabitants and visitors. The corral was outside the main wall, with the tops of its walls thickly planted with a thorny cactus to keep off Indian raiders.

The fort was so large that its staff averaged about eighty employees. Most of these were married, with Indian or Mexican wives. The fort had its own gardens, fields, and herds for a steady supply of fresh food.

Social life was limited, but story-telling was an agreeable way to spend an evening. Many of the men had remarkable stories, some true and some not. Checkers, cards, and billiards were the chief pastimes, and there were often dances.

It was a treat to have visitors from the East who could provide fairly up-to-date news of politics. Newspapers were scarce, turning up perhaps once or twice a year. Animal pets were common—some posts had peacocks brought from the Orient.

Many of these forts later became the sites of towns. The trend was foreshadowed by 1840, when the beaver trade had already surrendered first place to the flourishing trade in buffalo robes.

Nevertheless it was in the 1840's that the fur trade made its last and perhaps greatest contribution to American history. The "Oregon" problem (described on page 42) had continued to be a bone of contention between the United States and Great Britain. Attempts to settle the dispute in 1818 had failed; another attempt in 1828 failed also.

Slowly it became evident that actual residence in this vast territory would eventually settle the argument. Ever since the days of Lewis and Clark, the fur trade had continued to send the mountain men across the Rockies to the Oregon country. The trappers brought back an ever growing fund of information about landmarks and the best routes. They discovered and popularized South Pass, the best pathway through the Rockies.

When Frémont explored South Pass in 1842 on an official mission for the United States government, he took a force of mountain men with him. It was under their guidance that he described the most efficient way to reach the Oregon country by following the Oregon Trail.

The resulting wave of emigration brought ten thousand American pioneers to the Oregon country by 1846. By then they were clamoring for the huge section of present-day Washington that the English had claimed for decades. In fact, there were hotheads in the American ranks who wanted a good slice of British Columbia as well.

However, the negotiations of 1846 settled the border dispute by amicable compromise. The line between the United States and Canada was established at forty-nine degrees all the way to the Pacific coast.

Thus the vast Oregon country became United States territory. It was a triumph that had been made possible by the mountain men, who by now were no longer mountain men. Some were traders, some were scouts or Indian agents. Some were retired, some were dead. Their day was done.

4 THE MOUNTAIN MEN

TOGETHER WITH the cowboys, who appeared in the West at a later date, the mountain men share the distinction of being the most romantic figures in American history. Washington Irving described the mountain men as "hardy, lithe, vigorous, and active; extravagant in word, thought, and deed; daring of danger; prodigal of the present, and thoughtless of the future."

Life in the wilderness led them to take on Indian ways, until some called them "white Injuns." When an Oregon pioneer met Joe Meek for the first time, he was reminded of an Indian: he saw in Meek "the same wild, unsettled, watchful expression of the eye, the same unnatural gesticulation in conversation, the same unwillingness to use words when a sign, a contortion of the face or body, or movement of the hand will manifest thought; in standing, walking, reading, in all but complexion, he was an Indian."

The mountain man's life was often hard, dirty, and dangerous. Many a time he advanced without knowing what lay beyond the horizon. The mountains around him towered into the clouds, yet without having been there before he sought out the mountain passes with sure instinct.

The mountain man took his life in his hands whenever he got into a canoe, for who could tell what treacherous shoals, rocks, and currents might be encountered around the next bend? The danger of sudden Indian raids was so great that a sizable number of these daring men were killed in surprise attacks.

There were other dangers—starvation; accidents; wild animals; frostbite; quicksands. But there were compensations. Above all the mountain men exulted in feeling free from restraint, no longer subject to law and civilized custom. Controlled at every turn by only the imperious whims of nature, they convinced themselves that they had no master.

Many but not all of the mountain men were wild and lawless. Jed Smith, one of the most famous, was deeply religious. Some were well read, and no strangers to Shakespeare and the Bible. History, biography, and fine poetry were prime favorites with the ones who did read. A book was highly prized among the trappers and passed from hand to hand until it was too tattered to use any longer.

Wild as the mountain men often were, they had their good side too. A sense of justice and loyalty was among their virtues. The fact is they were highly contradictory people—generous and suspicious, kind and vengeful, easy-going and vigilant. Despite all the hardships of their lonely life, they loved the wilderness.

They were always restless, yet content with simple pleasures. Jim Clyman once rested in the shade of a cottonwood grove because it gave him so much pleasure to watch some martins near their nest. He enjoyed the gentle twittering of the birds—"It reminded me of home and civilisation."

George Frederick Ruxton, an English army officer who spent several enthralling years in the company of the mountain men, wrote admiringly of their explorations: "Not a hole or corner in the vast wilderness of the Far West but has been ransacked by these hardy men."

This impressive tribute cannot really be appreciated until we have a clear picture of the conditions of daily living among the mountain men. To begin with, they had to have many skills. (The actual techniques of trapping beaver will be described a little later on.)

The mountain man had to be a perfect shot. This in itself did not make him a perfect hunter; he also had to know the habits of wild animals, and how to butcher game and dress skins. He had to be expert in handling knife and ax, and in making canoes, snowshoes, or saddles.

He constructed forts, repaired guns. He was a teamster, a packer, a horse wrangler. He could trail for miles, following footprints and other signs. By the same token, he had the knack of hiding his tracks.

The trapper's life often depended on his familiarity with Indian customs; even more important was his understanding of how the Indian's mind worked. Memory was important too. Many trappers—Kit Carson, for example—had photographic memories that made it possible for them to recognize the most trifling landmark even after the passage of fifteen years.

The trapper had to have a smattering of many languages —Mexican Spanish and French Canadian dialect, as well as the tongues of the Plains Indians and mountain Indians. The mountain man also mastered the sign language of the Plains Indians, which served well for an amazing variety of ideas.

Possessing all these skills, the trapper naturally thought well of himself, and also respected his comrades who had likewise acquired these skills. These attitudes were in the last analysis the source of the democratic spirit found among the mountain men. But theirs was a rather enclosed world, and occasionally they made discoveries that shocked them.

For example, at one trappers' rendezvous the mountain men met an English nobleman who dressed like a fop. He wore a white shooting jacket, colorful shepherd's plaids, and a Panama hat, and carried an elegant fowling piece. The trappers laughed and laughed—never had they seen such a ludicrous outfit or such a strange firearm.

Even more outlandish to them was his elaborate gear. He had wagons piled with the finest hams and tongues, tins of meats and other delicacies, jars of pickles, choice wines, the best brands of tea and coffee, plenty of sugar, and barrels of flour. To top it off, he had his meals served by his servants on an exquisite silver service.

When the trappers were not guffawing, they gaped in simple wonder. Such luxuries were beyond their imagining, let alone their knowledge. How could such a dude get along in the wilderness?

But soon their ridicule turned to respect and liking. The Englishman was a magnificent rider. He was as good a shot as the most expert trapper. And when it came to skirmishing with the Indians, he was just as brave and cool as the most experienced mountain men. Best of all, he was delightfully hospitable and took pleasure in sharing all his supplies with the trappers. And they in turn were so democratic that they accepted even an aristocrat on equal terms.

The vigil against Indian attack had to go on unceasingly. A trapper named William Waldo left one of the most vivid descriptions of what it meant to live in Indian country. About one of his trips that lasted seven weeks, he wrote that his men rarely got more than three or four hours' sleep out of the twenty-four. Soon they were so worn out by the combination of working during the day and standing guard at night that they began to go to sleep and fall to the ground while riding.

During this whole time, they were ordered to keep their clothes and boots on every night. They slept uneasily with pistols in their belts and rifles cradled in their arms. Sometimes, while they were fast asleep, men grabbed their own knives spasmodically and drove them into the ground. Soon they became afraid of killing one another in their sleep. It is easy to imagine the relief with which they got back to safety once more.

The older French Canadian trapper generally lived in a cabin and was supplied with food from not-too-distant settlements. Not so the American trapper. He lived in a tent or rolled himself up in a blanket outdoors. When he was hungry he shot his game and cooked it with his own hands at his own fire. This kind of life accounted to some extent for his fierce spirit of independence.

The French trapper lived in comparative ease with his Indian wife and relished some of the minor comforts of civilization. He was content to follow his leader's orders and advice.

The American trapper was more of a lone wolf. Solitude had no terrors for him. "Drop him in the midst of a prairie, or in the heart of the mountains, and he is never at a loss. He notices every landmark; can retrace his route through the most monotonous plains, or the most perplexed labyrinths of the mountains; no danger nor difficulty can appall him, and he scorns to complain under any privation."

Yet many trappers, as they got older, began to hanker for some of the comforts of home. When they married Indian girls, they became honorary members of the tribe. This gave them many Indian friends, of course, but it also brought them into conflict with the Indian enemies of the tribe.

In the wintertime the mountain man's life was particularly hard. Trapping was out of the question. The men built themselves stout tepees of deer and elk skin, and sat out the winter while the beavers hibernated in their lodges. Holed up in a snug valley, the trapper was safe from storms and reasonably secure from Indian hunting parties. (There was little game about at that time of the year.) The area had to be well grassed and wooded to provide food for the horses and mules.

With the coming of spring the beaver streams thawed out enough for more trapping. The mountain men would be glad to be outdoors by then; during the winter they had been saved from danger, though not from boredom.

Much worse than such an uneventful season was the unwelcome prospect of having to make a winter trip. Jim Beckwourth, a famous trapper, tells of a grim expedition into the mountain country in the winter of 1824. The snow was deep, the winds cutting, and the cold so severe that some of the horses froze to death.

Under such conditions travelers need a great deal of nourishing food. All the trappers had, however, was a daily allowance per man of half a pint of flour, which was made into an unappetizing gruel. Occasionally someone managed to kill a goose or duck, which was divided up into equal though tiny shares.

"A duller encampment, I suppose, never was witnessed," Beckwourth writes. "No jokes, no fireside stories, no fun; each man rose in the morning with the gloom of the preceding night filling his mind; we built our fires and partook of our scanty repast without saying a word."

But this was luxurious living in comparison to what happened on Frémont's unfortunate attempt to cross the Rockies in the dead of winter. Here is a passage from Thomas E. Breckenridge's account:

"Our frozen feet soon gave out. We were compelled to get down on our hands and knees. For nearly the entire distance we crawled on ice or through snow. Before half the distance was covered, our remnants of blankets had been used to wrap around frozen limbs. Our suffering was almost beyond description. Those who have been affected with snow-blindness can appreciate our situation.

"Our feet had been so frozen and thawed that the flesh began to come off. It was a painful operation to dress those horrible sores. We were obliged to use day after day the same old pieces of woolen blankets covered with deer's tallow. Truly that last forty miles was a trail of blood. It required ten days to reach the settlement—ten days of the most excruciating pain. Looking back, after so many years, I cannot understand how we lived through it."

Wintertime also brought the danger of starving because game was scarce then. More than one story was told of desperate mountain men eating their moccasins in milder seasons when nothing else was available in the way of food.

So hunting meant something quite different to the mountain man than it does to the modern sportsman. For the trapper, hunting was literally a matter of life and death. If he found game, he ate well. If he had a bad day, he went hungry.

If the modern hunter takes aim and misses, he is merely annoyed. As for the trapper, he had to be a good shot or he might starve to death. And his supply of ammunition had to last, no matter how much longer he had to stay in the mountains beyond his original expectations! Hence the irregularity of his mealtimes: he ate when he was hungry— and when he had food.

For the most part the trappers lived off the country. As we have seen, they shared the Indians' preference for buffalo meat above all other foods. The mountain men also liked bear, elk, antelope, panther, and deer meat. According to some, beaver tail was a delicacy second only to buffalo meat.

Like the Indians, the mountain men took keen pleasure

in the excitement of a buffalo hunt. Ruxton, who had a share in several of these hunts, painted a graphic picture of the death throes of a wounded buffalo:

"A bull, shot through the heart or lungs, with blood streaming from his mouth, and protruding tongue, his eyes rolling, bloodshot, and glazed with death, braces himself on his legs, swaying from side to side, stamps impatiently at his growing weakness, or lifts his rugged and matted head and helplessly bellows out his conscious impotence. To the last, however, he endeavors to stand upright and plants his limbs farther apart, but to no purpose. As the body rolls like a ship at sea, his head slowly turns from side to side, looking about, as it were, for the unseen and treacherous enemy who has brought him, the lord of the plains, to such a pass.

"Gouts of purple blood spurt from his mouth and nostrils, and gradually the failing limbs refuse longer to support the ponderous carcass; more heavily rolls the body from side to side until suddenly, for a brief instant, it becomes rigid and still; a convulsive tremor seizes it and, with a low, sobbing gasp, the huge animal falls over on his side, the limbs extended stark and stiff, and the mountain of flesh without life or motion."

The mountain men's tastes in dress were greatly influenced by the Indians. Most trappers wore a cotton or flannel shirt; calico with ruffles was the occasional choice of dandies. Buckskins, often elaborately ornamented, were more lasting. But when they dried out after rain, they could be as stiff as a coat of armor.

The buckskin fringes, which we think of as purely decorative, had a definitely practical value as far as the trapper was concerned: fringes helped the rain to run off. They were also useful in the making of patches, known in trappers' lingo as "whangs." After eating, trappers always wiped their knives dry on their clothes. This was delightfully convenient, and the grease helped waterproof their garments. Almost every observant description of trappers alludes to the greasy appearance of their clothes.

Leather breeches, leggings made of blanket material or buffalo skin, and moccasins of buffalo, elk, or deer skin completed the trapper's basic costume. The leggings and moccasins were richly embroidered in the Indian manner.

For a coat he wore a brightly colored blanket (like the Indians and Mexicans), or else a buffalo robe. His pipe was fashioned like an Indian pipe.

The trapper wore his hair long, either letting it fall over his shoulders or else braiding it neatly, Indian style. He wore a hat or knotted kerchief over his head as protection from the sun and insects.

On horseback, the mountain man always held his rifle in front of him as he rode. His gun—literally his best friend —was decorated with brass tacks and patches of vermilion and kept in a cover adorned with fringes and some feathers.

Almost as important to the mountain man was his horse, the faithful companion of all his dangerous experiences. The horse was a choice animal, carefully selected for speed and intelligence. It was richly ornamented, down to the streaks of white clay or vermilion that were daubed on by way of dashing contrast to the animal's color. The trapper generally had one or two pack horses or mules. Each animal carried a burden of about two hundred pounds, including the trapper's "possible" bag, containing his cooking utensils, food, tobacco, bedding, and assorted odds and ends. He generally slept in the open on a buffalo robe, perhaps bedded down on boughs and leaves, with his saddle for a pillow.

To Ruxton we owe the classic description of one of the most picturesque of all the mountain men: Old Bill Williams, whose life is described in Chapter Six:

"Williams always rode ahead, his body bent over his saddle-horn, across which rested a long heavy rifle, his keen gray eyes peering from under the slouched brim of a flexible felt hat, black and shining with grease. His buckskin hunting shirt, bedaubed until it had the appearance of polished leather, hung in folds over his bony carcass."

Old Bill also wore "pantaloons of the same material with scattered fringes down the outside of the leg." Rain and wading had shrunk them so that they "clung tightly to his long, spare, sinewy legs. His feet were thrust into a pair of Mexican stirrups made of wood, and as big as coal scuttles. Iron spurs of incredible proportions, with tinkling drops attached to the rowels, were fastened to his heel— a bead-worked strap, four inches broad, secured them over the instep.

"In the shoulder belt which sustained his powder horn and bullet pouch, were fastened the various instruments essential to one pursuing his mode of life. An awl, with deer-horn handle, and the point defended by a case of cherry wood carved by his own hand, hung at the back of the belt. . . . Under this was a squat and quaint-looking bullet mould, the handles guarded by strips of buckskin [and] having for its companion a little bottle made from the point of an antelope's horn, scraped transparent, which contained the medicine used in baiting the traps."

The mountain man had to be the master of a hundred skills. But above all, he had to know how to trap beaver.

Beavers live in or near streams. They average thirty-five pounds in weight, though some range as high as fifty or sixty pounds. Their hind feet are webbed, and they have a scaly tail that occasionally acts as a sculling organ when they swim. The tail is remarkably versatile, for it affords good balance when the animal is running and also makes it easy for the beaver to squat on its haunches. Some observers have claimed that this creature warns fellow-beavers of danger by loudly slapping the water with its tail.

Beavers eat bark and the leaves of trees, which they gnaw with their remarkably sharp teeth. They live on swift streams and also in quiet waters. On the latter they build a home of branches and twigs plastered together with mud. In swift-running streams beavers construct a tunnel to the bank of the river and then build their lodges above water level.

Beaver traps were made of iron and weighed about five pounds apiece. A trapper carried at the most six traps, together with his rifle, a hatchet, a blanket, and a knife for skinning. He also had to have his powder horn and lead shot for the rifle.

Trappers worked in pairs, each one taking one side of a stream. They sheltered themselves with "huts" made of boughs and left open at the side facing the campfire. By putting up racks of poles or antlers, they made places to hang meat, traps, and clothes.

The trappers were highly skilled when it came to finding signs of beaver in the neighborhood. They might see a beaver slide to the water, or find the animal's tracks in the mud. Perhaps they might catch sight of the beaver's lodge in the water, or else glimpse a dam built by the industrious animal. Gnawed or torn bark on the river bank would be another sign. In all such cases the trapper knew it was worth while to set his trap.

Instead of walking along the side of the stream, trappers often made their way through the water, even if it was ice cold. In this way they avoided leaving a telltale scent that would warn the beaver of their presence.

Setting the traps in place in fairly shallow water was not too hard, but when placing the trap in much deeper water the mountain man was often up to his neck in near-freezing water. Worse yet, he had to keep moving in the water at least a quarter of a mile before he approached the river bank. If he left the water at once after setting the trap, his scent might be noticed by nearby beaver.

Many a trapper died from exposure in the icy mountain streams. There were occasional accidents from treacherous currents and from hidden snags and stones. In working on fairly large streams, trappers often used dugouts and saved themselves a great deal of misery.

When the trapper had picked a likely spot in the stream for his trap, he took it out from his pack and placed it underwater near the bank. Its powerful metal jaws were open. The five-foot iron chain of the trap was fastened to

a tree or stump on shore. Sometimes a long, smooth stake was fastened to the stream bottom, and the chain moved along this stake as far as a fork fashioned toward the bottom of the stake.

The bait was castor, a powerful-smelling secretion from the beaver's perineal gland. This bait had an irresistible attraction for any beavers in the vicinity. The trapper smeared it over the top of a small twig. The bottom end of the twig was fastened to the trap, while the smeared end protruded about four inches above the surface. The trapper's last step was to attach to the trap a long string with some kind of marker that floated free on the water.

When a beaver sniffed the bait, he would come close to it. One of his paws touched the trap, which snapped shut on the paw. The panicky animal struggled to escape. This pulled the chain down so that it got stuck in the fork. It was no longer possible for the beaver to reach the surface, and the trapped animal was drowned.

Next day at dawn the trapper would go back, search for the floating markers, and find the bodies. He would skin the beavers on the spot and bring the pelts into camp, where they would be stretched on a frame, scraped, dried, and folded with the fur side in. Beaver pelts were pressed into standard packs of eighty skins tied tightly with buckskin thongs.

The cache, or hiding place, was an important part of trapping. There were times when trappers found it useful to hide away furs or supplies or both. Perhaps they feared Indian attack. Or else they might be coming to difficult terrain and were short of pack animals. Then they would dig out a cache, coming back to the hiding place months later in some cases.

Making a cache was an art. Firm, solidly packed soil near a stream was the proper location. The trappers dug out some sod and spread it neatly on buffalo robes. Then they dug a hole, as narrow as possible at the top and much wider underneath. All the earth taken out was also spread on buffalo robes and then carted away to the stream. The idea was to avoid leaving the slightest trace of any excavating.

Coming back to the cache, the trappers would line it with leaves and branches and then pack in the furs and supplies. Then came a covering of more branches and possibly straw, topped with a smooth layer of earth. Finally the sod was restored with the utmost care.

By keeping their horses tethered at the spot for several days, the trappers covered up the cache with many confusing hoof marks. And, before they departed, they made a campfire on the site, charring the surface and covering it with ashes.

What could have been more painstaking? Yet the trappers' stories give one instance after another of crafty Indian discoveries of a cache! Sometimes the hiding place remained undiscovered, and the trappers would dig it up exultantly —only to find that the contents had been damaged by the seepage of underground water. It was just one more hazard of the tantalizing fur trade.

There were two main trapping seasons: in the spring, from the thaws until summer set in, and from the end of September until the streams turned icy in the fall. In the summer months, when the beaver shed his thick fur, trapping would have been pointless. And during the dead of winter the beaver lived snug and safe behind his barrier of frozen mud and cunningly arranged logs.

So for half the year trapping was out of the question. Many a trapper used the slack period to cultivate his social life. He might get together with other trappers in their favorite haunts. If he had an Indian wife, he would tinker about his lodge or log cabin, repairing and doing odd jobs; or he might pay a long sociable visit to his in-laws.

In the summertime the trappers found other ways to make a living. They served as guides or scouts with wagon trains or hunted game for a trading post. Catching wild horses was another suitable occupation.

Even during the slack season, trappers rarely went back to St. Louis. Jim Bridger once confessed that he had not tasted bread for seventeen years! For most trappers the great event of the year was the rendezvous held at Pierre's Hole in northeastern Idaho after the spring season. This was a combination trade fair and jamboree at which the free trappers disposed of their furs, laid in new supplies, and had an uproarious good time.

Each company had an annual rendezvous where trappers, hunters, traders, half-breeds, and Indians awaited the coming of supplies from the East. For the trappers there were guns, powder, traps, coffee, tea, sugar, tobacco, and liquor. For the Indians there were such trade goods as arms and ammunition, utensils, blankets, shawls, colored cloth, bright trinkets, and the like.

On these occasions the Indians were sometimes friends, sometimes foes. Since they greatly outnumbered the trappers, the Indians could not always resist the opportunity for sudden attack. They might bring in their furs peacefully for friendly trade; or they might attack a band of trappers, kill them, and take their furs. Or, most likely, the Indians might combine the arts of war and peace. The result was an uneasy truce occasionally marred by a sudden flare of anger.

There was always a race between the companies to see who could bring in the supplies first, get the choicest furs, and make the fastest start for the next season. Interestingly enough, most of the hardware and cloth goods came from England, relatively little from the United States. (At that time, British workmanship and materials were generally superior—and cheaper, too.) Thus there was an intimate connection between the men who worked at humdrum jobs in the mills of Manchester and the factories of Sheffield and the lonely men who roamed the wilderness across the sea.

Beaver fur was the currency of the frontier. A standard beaver pelt weighed a pound and a half or more and averaged five dollars in value. The French Canadian term for a pelt was *plus*, or in trappers' talk a "plew." The trade goods were unconscionably overvalued by the companies, so that the trappers paid one plew for a pint of whiskey or a pound of gunpowder or coffee. The price of a good blanket was in the neighborhood of fifteen plews!

Thus most of the proceeds of the trappers' hard, dangerous work went into supplies for the coming year, as well as gewgaws for their Indian wives and sweethearts. What was left over they spent on having a riotous good time—

feasts, dancing, storytelling, horse races, shooting contests, foot racing, wrestling, drinking, and brawling.

In their more sedate moments the mountain men told tall tales—the taller the better. Boasting, exaggeration, and elaborate lying were the order of the day. In this short time of feverishly wild social life many a trapper had his only relief from a whole year of loneliness, tension, and danger.

No one ever became rich from trapping. In the heyday of the fur trade the highest price for a plew was six dollars. And this price was not really high, because the prices of trappers' supplies were astronomical.

By the end of the 1830's the best beaver streams were becoming exhausted, and the beaver hat was slumping badly in popularity as headgear of silk and other materials replaced it. The price of plews plummeted disastrously to a dollar apiece. The trapper was no businessman, but at that point he realized that the beaver trade had seen its best days, and that it was time for him to find another way to make a living. Thus the mountain man disappeared from the stage of history.

So far we have described the mountain men as a group. Individuals have not stood out. Actually, each mountain man was very decidedly himself, and like no one else in the world. In the following chapters we learn something about the most colorful trappers, and about the wondering and admiring tales that were told of them around many a lonely campfire.

5 JOHN COLTER

NOWADAYS, WHEN someone tells us about the wonders of Yellowstone National Park, we are quite ready to believe him. We are astonished but not skeptical to learn that the area has some three thousand geysers and hot springs. When we hear that Old Faithful spouts a column of water almost 150 feet high about once every 65 minutes, our reaction is, "Gosh! I'd like to see that for myself!"

It's harder to believe that Yellowstone has a Grasshopper Glacier where you can see millions of grasshoppers that were frozen in thousands of years ago. We wonder how they got there, but we don't doubt that they *are* there.

But that is by no means the reception that was given to John Colter, the first white man who saw the wonders of Yellowstone. People either roundly called him a liar or else marveled at his fertile imagination. And yet his story is well worth knowing, for it is connected with some of the most exciting adventures that ever befell a mountain man.

John Colter was born in Virginia in 1775, the opening year of the American Revolution. His parents died while he was a child, and he went to live with an aunt and uncle.

Farming bored him. He was a good shot, and loved hunting and the solitude of the forest. As he grew older he became more and more restless and unwilling to settle down and raise a family. Often he thought with longing of visiting the Far West, at that time as little known as the interior of Africa. Colter was approaching his thirties when, one day in 1803, he heard that two regular army officers named Lewis and Clark were planning to explore the unknown country between the Mississippi River and the Oregon coast.

Immediately afire with enthusiasm, Colter applied for a place in the expedition. He was readily accepted, for he was powerfully built, an excellent hunter, and a skilled woodsman. Thus Colter became one of the first white men to journey west from the banks of the Mississippi across the Rockies and on to the shores of the Pacific. They crossed the endlessly rolling prairies, traveled along rivers that were turbulent and sluggish by turns, crept through snowy mountain passes, knew hunger, thirst, and weariness, and had many an anxious moment with strange Indians. Yet, despite the absence of any accurate map, they covered thousands of miles of wilderness and returned safe and successful.

On the return trip Colter met two trappers named Dixon and Hancock who were hunting beaver along the Yellowstone River. They asked him to join them. It was an attractive notion. After three years in the wilderness, Colter had little taste for the quiet life back home.

Receiving permission from his commanders to leave the expedition, Colter turned to trapping beaver with his new associates. He knew that he was facing danger and hardship and possible death. Three men would have little chance against hostile Indians. But the lure of the wilderness was irresistible.

To buy supplies, Colter had more money than he had ever seen in his life—the $179.33 he had earned in three years with the expedition. When winter came Colter holed up with his new-found friends in a snug shelter for a while. But time hung heavy on his hands, and one day he calmly set out for a trip over the snowdrifts.

In order to be able to find his way back, Colter carved

his initials on rocks and trees. From time to time he would drop in at Indian villages. During the exploring trip he had learned the universal sign language of the Indians and had picked up a smattering of Indian dialects.

This was enough to make himself understood. When he arrived at a village he made peace signs to show that he came as a friend. And, bloodthirsty and savage though the Indians might be, they never harmed him. They treated him hospitably and gave him food and shelter. In fact, the Indians' code of courtesy called for sending along a brave to guide Colter to the next village.

Toward the end of winter Colter returned to his friends, and they trapped together all spring. When the trapping season was over they divided up their beaver pelts, for Colter was more determined than ever to work by himself. His partners thought this was folly, but they respected his decision.

After some weeks of wandering, Colter ran into a party of thirty-seven trappers headed by Manuel Lisa, the first large-scale fur trader in the trans-Mississippi country. After some talk about their prospects, Lisa took Colter on as a "free trapper." Colter would trap by himself and be his own boss, but he would trade his pelts to Lisa. He would also hunt for the group. At the same time he would benefit by being part of a large expedition of well-armed, skilled frontiersmen. It seemed a good deal for all concerned.

In the fall the party reached the mouth of the Big Horn

River (in present-day Wyoming), where they built a post called Fort Raymond. Before the fort was finished Lisa called on Colter for a dangerous mission. He wanted Colter to travel some five hundred miles in the snow to the land of the Crow Indians (in southern present-day Montana). Colter was to tell the Crows about the new trading post and get them to bring in their pelts for trading.

Setting out on foot, Colter took a gun, a blanket, a pair of snowshoes, and a thirty-pound pack filled with presents for the Indians. Fantastic as it may sound, he made his way through the snow-covered wilderness so efficiently that he eventually reached the first Crow village he had visited the previous winter.

The Crows remembered him. In fact they gave him a delighted welcome and staged a great feast in his honor. He had no trouble persuading them to trade at Lisa's post. Going on to one Crow village after another, he succeeded each time in getting the Indians to agree to trade with Lisa—and this despite the fact that Colter was the first white man they had ever seen.

At last he came to a village where the Indians told him he would have to turn back. If he went any farther, they warned, he would find himself in the dwelling place of evil spirits. No Indian dared venture there.

Despite the well-meant advice of the Indians, Colter insisted on going ahead. Any hint of risk only whetted his eagerness to go on. At last he came to a large, beautiful lake—Yellowstone Lake, in the northwest corner of present-day Wyoming. The country was breathtaking in its wild splendor but bare of any traces of human beings. Colter was not only the first white man to see it; few Indians had been there before him.

Soon Colter knew the reason why. There were places where the earth trembled. In the dead of winter hot springs hissed out of the ground. In other places he saw pools with water that was blackened by an oozing, tarlike substance. To the Indians this all meant that Yellowstone Valley was bewitched, the abode of baleful spirits.

With awe and fascination, and perhaps not a little fear, Colter kept right on. Never had he encountered a scene of such overpowering grandeur. Suddenly he stopped as he heard a strange rumble, and without any more warning a huge spurt of water gushed high up out of the ground.

Months later, Colter returned to Lisa's band. When he told them of the weird sights he had seen in Yellowstone Valley, they laughed until tears streamed from their eyes. Colter, they all agreed, had a stock of the tallest tales any frontiersman had ever invented. Then and there they named his "imaginary" region "Colter's Hell."

When Lisa and his trappers returned to St. Louis, Colter did not go with them. Lisa had given him an even more dangerous assignment—to visit the hostile Blackfeet and try to persuade them to trade at the new post. On the way he paid another visit to the Crows, who had pleasant memories of his earlier visits and gave him a hospitable reception.

This time the Crows were encamped with another friendly tribe, the Flatheads. The village with its many rows of tepees was full of din and bustle. The men had a good time with athletic contests, dancing, storytelling, and gambling games, while the women worked industriously at many tasks.

Colter enjoyed himself hugely, and each day proved more delightful than the one before. But one day there was a grim end to the festivities. With no warning a great war party of mounted Blackfoot warriors descended on the camp. They were a terrifying sight, with their long head-dresses and hideous war paint. In full gallop they came on swiftly, screaming and brandishing their weapons.

There were over a thousand Blackfeet in this band. Though hopelessly outnumbered, the Crows and Flatheads fought back hard. Colter, as a white man and a neutral, took no part in the fighting at first. But this was no time for neutrality, for he was trapped. An arrow wounded him badly in the thigh, and, though he was almost maddened by the pain, Colter realized that he had no alternative but to fight.

His rifle brought down many an enemy on this battle-field where both sides were still equipped with bow and arrow. The Blackfeet, seeing what was happening, venge-fully marked Colter out for special treatment. However, he had a miraculous escape: just as it seemed that the Black-

feet were about to triumph, a large band of Crows galloped up and drove them away.

The battle between the Crows and the Blackfeet ended Colter's hopes of visiting that tribe. They knew him now for an enemy, and he would do well to keep a healthy distance from them. Although his wound was still painful, he decided to ride back to Fort Raymond. There he would be safe, and his wound could be treated fairly effectively.

He knew the trip would be difficult. The danger from Indian attack would be greater than ever, and the constant jogging of the horseback ride would trouble him because of his wound.

As Colter feared, the trip proved long, slow, and painful. He proceeded with great caution, always on the lookout for stray bands of hostile braves. But at last he arrived safely at Fort Raymond. Here his wound healed so slowly that Colter found it hard to put up with inactive life indoors.

Finally in late autumn he went trapping on the Jefferson River (in southwestern present-day Montana) with John Potts, who had offered to work with him. Despite all their caution they could not avoid the Blackfeet. One morning, as they were paddling down the river, they rounded a bend—and found seven hundred Blackfeet on shore!

Colter saw it was pointless to resist, and surrendered at once. He might be able to talk his way out of the trap; fighting was of course quite hopeless. No sooner was he on shore than the Indians took away his weapons and his clothes.

As for Potts, he rashly decided to go down fighting. He killed one Indian before he was felled by scores of arrows. Howling triumphantly, the Indians chopped his body to pieces.

Every moment Colter expected to be butchered in the same hideous way, but the slaughter had evidently put the Indians in a playful mood. Giving Colter a head start of a few hundred yards, about five hundred warriors began chasing him. Whoever caught up with him first would earn the honor of killing and scalping him.

It was an Indian's idea of grand sport, but Colter was

determined to spoil the fun if he could. We have been told that he was a man of exceptional endurance. Running in a country where the sharp spines of the prickly pear cruelly pierced his bare feet, he ran as he had never run before. At first he expected to be overtaken momentarily, but when he looked back after about three miles, he saw that he had outdistanced all but a few of his pursuers.

One Indian, the best racer of the lot, began to gain strongly on him. Colter's lungs felt as if they were about to burst, and his nose was bleeding heavily as he breathed in great wracking sobs and gulps. The sound of his pursuer's pounding footsteps became louder and louder.

At last, when the Indian was nearly upon him, Colter suddenly whirled about. The sight of the blood-spattered

white man unnerved the Indian. Quick as a flash, Colter grabbed the Indian's spear and thrust it through him. Then he snatched up the Indian's blanket and dashed for a grove of trees on the river bank.

Here Colter, momentarily out of the enemy's sight, was able to rest for a while. Then he plunged into the river and swam out to a tangled pile of driftwood. The enraged Indians spent hours in vain search for him until they at last gave up the man hunt.

But Colter was still far from safe. Unarmed, and naked except for the blanket, he had little protection against the elements and none against prowling animals. It took him seven days to stagger the thirty miles to Fort Raymond, and in all that time he had nothing to eat but roots. At last he reached his goal, utterly worn out and covered from head to foot with scars and scratches.

Although other mountain men performed heroic deeds and had narrow escapes, Colter was one of the first on the scene. And during many an evening of yarn-spinning under the stars, the mountain men told and retold the wonderful stories of "Colter's Hell" and John Colter's miraculous escape from the bloodthirsty Blackfeet.

But that was not the only legacy that Colter left to the men who came after him. Without meaning to, he had started the feud with the Blackfeet that plagued the mountain men long after Colter had left the scene of his famous exploits.

6 OLD BILL WILLIAMS

His Indian friends called him "Lone Elk." He was christened, sedately enough, William Sherley Williams. But to the mountain men he was always "Old Bill." Having come West much earlier than such famous trappers as Kit Carson and Jim Bridger, he was an old man when they were in their prime.

Little is known of his childhood and youth. We know he was born in Rutherford County, North Carolina, in 1787. As a young man he emigrated to Missouri with his family. For a while he was a traveling Methodist preacher —a strange background for his later career. There is a story that he fell in love with a girl who made fun of him. He was so humiliated that he left home and went West. This is supposed to have happened about 1822, roughly a decade before the heyday of the fur trade.

In the years that followed, there was hardly a spot in all the Far West that Bill Williams left unexplored. He is mentioned as hunting and trapping and acting as a guide in Texas, on the Santa Fe Trail, on the route to California, and of course in the Rocky Mountain country.

Old Bill lived with one Indian tribe or another for many years, and adopted their ways and their languages. At one period of his life he was away from civilization for twenty-one years! His knowledge proved helpful to missionaries sent to convert the Indians.

The padres in the old Spanish missions admired Bill's familiarity with Indian lore. They were very fond of him, despite his indifference to religion. He helped them translate the Scriptures into Indian languages, dryly commenting that while the Bible would do the Indians no good, it would do them no harm either. Yet wherever Bill went, he carried a Bible and a volume of Shakespeare with him.

He had a reputation for being scrupulous in his dealings with Indians, although their haggling exasperated him. On one occasion he became so angry that he set fire to his trade goods and went off into the wilderness for six months. And yet if he saw a trader taking advantage of the Indians, his rage boiled over, and he would protest hotly. In one such dispute he hit the offender so hard that the man did not recover consciousness for an hour.

As a man who lived a solitary life, Williams rarely saw children. However, he loved their company: something about them charmed away his self-centered brooding and his sardonic attitude toward the world. Once, when he was near a Ute band decked out in war paint, he found a Ute infant who had been lost in a gully. Without hesitating a moment, he picked up the child in his arms and, at the risk of his life, brought it to the Indians' camp. They were so touched by his kind action that they allowed him to persuade them in the full flush of his momentarily peaceful mood to forsake the warpath.

In the opinion of a man who knew many of the famous trappers, Bill "was the bravest and most fearless mountaineer of all; the tribes from the Mexican border to the Canadian knew him and feared him, thinking perhaps he was some supernatural being."

Another memorable description comes from Albert Pike, who met Bill in 1832:

"As a specimen of the original trapper, Bill Williams certainly stands foremost. He is a man of about six feet one inch in height, gaunt and red-headed, with a hard, weather-beaten face, marked deeply with the smallpox. He is all muscle and sinew, and the most indefatigable hunter and trapper in the world.

"He has no glory except in the woods, and his ambition is to kill more deer and catch more beaver than any other man about him. Nothing tires him, not even running all day with six traps on his back. . . . Neither is he a fool. He is a shrewd, acute, original man, and far from illiterate."

Bill's temper was uncertain, as we have seen, and it led him to do weird things. Once, when he was about forty-five years old, he went into a restaurant in Taos, New Mexico. This was a favorite haunt of the Southwestern trappers. When Bill asked the cook whether he had anything to eat, the cook replied politely (in Spanish) that he did not understand English. By way of reply, Old Bill grasped the poor man, lifted him up, and kicked him into the kitchen. And, what is perhaps more revealing than anything else about this incident, the two later became good friends!

Like most of the mountain men, Bill had no use for money. Though he obtained his beaver pelts by the hardest kind of work and at daily risk of his life, he was content to squander his earnings on a good time. Micajah McGee, who knew Bill well, tells this characteristic story:

"He once came into Taos and spent on one spree six thousand dollars, the result of a successful season of trapping, and then left the place in debt. One of his amusements on this occasion was to buy whole bolts of calico, then quite a costly article in Taos, and, going into the street, to take hold of one end and throw out the other as far as he could, unrolling it on the ground, and then call out the Mexican women to scramble for it. In this way, and with drinking and gambling, three or four weeks would suffice to run through his money."

It was not in Old Bill's restless nature to retire some day, sitting comfortably in a rocking chair and staring placidly at the peaceful countryside somewhere in "the States." Instead, he remained tirelessly active to the end.

In his later years he preferred to be by himself as a rule, and often traveled without companions even in the most dangerous Indian country. Hence his nickname, Lone Elk. (Old Bill believed in reincarnation, and thought he would be reborn as an elk.)

Though most mountain men sensibly believed there was safety in numbers, he would often leave a large group when he sniffed the possibility of Indian attack. "Do'ee hyar now, boys, thar's sign about?" he would quaver in his high-pitched voice. "This hoss feels like caching [hiding]." And off he would go, despite the arguments of his companions.

In his old age Bill staggered rather than walked, moving first to one side and then to the other. When he lifted his rifle it trembled in his hands, yet he was still a notable shot. He had been in many a scrape with hostile Indians and was a notorious scalp-lifter.

Old Bill was now scrawny, worn yet tough. His face was sharp and wrinkled, and he had jaws like a nutcracker. He spoke like the mountain man he was, favoring expressions like "oncet," "haint gotter," "plumb," and "varmint."

In his unforgettable description of Old Bill, George Frederick Ruxton wrote that "his head was always bent forward, giving him the appearance of being hump-backed. He *appeared* to look neither to the right nor left, but, in fact, his little twinkling eye was everywhere. He looked at no one he was addressing, always seeming to be thinking of something else than the subject of his discourse, speaking in a whining, thin, cracked voice, and in a tone that left the hearer in doubt whether he was laughing or crying."

About this time Old Bill went on a trapping expedition in the Yellowstone region with some friends. One night he dreamed that God Almighty appeared before him, "in flames and sparkling flashes of fire." In this vision the Lord said to him: "Williams, you have been a very wicked man. I have saved your life very often, and you have not profited by it, but I will save you once more."

Just then the sound of gunfire was heard—a surprise attack by Indians! Many of the trappers were killed in their sleep, but Old Bill grabbed his knife and gun and escaped with his life.

Asked later whether he had profited by his dream, Old Bill replied, "Well, I don't know; I've worked very hard at my traps, and paid all my debts; I've given up swearing and that sort o' thing, and if I knew anything else I'd do it."

It was too late. A little while afterward, at the age of sixty-two, he was killed in a Ute ambush in the Southwest.

An Indian who had known Old Bill well summed up his somber life in these eloquent words, quoted by Colonel Frank Triplett:

" 'He was a great hunter, a great trapper—took many beaver, and a great warrior—his belt was full of scalps; but no friend; no squaw; always by himself'—here he separated his thumb as far as possible from his fingers, to express his loneliness—'like the eagle in the heavens, or the panther on the mountain. He was not a talkative man and those with whom he mingled, judged of his deeds only by his new scars and the fresh scalps at his girdle.' "

7 JED SMITH

LIKE OLD BILL WILLIAMS, Jed Smith died at the hands of Indians in a treacherous attack. But whereas Williams was an old man when he was murdered, Jed died at the age of thirty-two. In less than ten short years he had managed to become one of the outstanding mountain men and perhaps the most widely respected trader in the business.

Jedediah Strong Smith was born of New England stock in Bainbridge, a small town in New York State, in 1799. He had little schooling, but a doctor in the town taught him reading and writing and also some Latin and English literature. Later on, the grateful pupil helped provide for his teacher's old age.

When the boy was thirteen he became a clerk on a Great Lakes freighter. But, as with many youngsters of his time, the spell of the West lured him irresistibly to St. Louis, and eleven years later he joined the famous Ashley expedition of a hundred trappers who were to ascend the Missouri and make their way across the Rockies.

Jed was twenty-four at the time. Though he had no experience as a trapper, he had many excellent qualities. He was powerfully built and exceptionally courageous. He was brave but not reckless, a good comrade with all the qualifications that make a fine leader. He had unusual gifts of endurance, and he was cool and resourceful in a crisis. His word could be relied upon; he was no empty boaster; and he had a deep sense of responsibility.

It took Jed three years to become a master trapper, learning all the tricks of woodcraft, becoming familiar with the ways of Indians, and tirelessly absorbing everything that was known of the trapper's lore. Like all the mountain men he had many a narrow escape from Indians, grizzlies, and other perils.

Once he was nearly killed by a grizzly that jumped out of a thicket and sprang on him, breaking several ribs and cutting his head severely. Jim Clyman, one of the trappers who was with him, has left us an account that is remarkable for its vivid matter-of-factness as well as its wayward spelling and complete disregard of punctuation:

"Grissly did not hesitate a moment but sprang on the capt taking him by the head first pitc[h]ing sprawling on the earth he gave him a grap by the middle fortunately catc[h]ing by the ball pouch and Butcher K[n]ife which he broke but breaking several ribs and cutting his head

badly none of us having any sugical Knowledge what was
to be done one Said come take hold and he wuld say why
not you so it went around   I asked the Cpt what was
best   he said one or 2 [go] for water and if you have a
needle and thread git it out and sew up my wounds around
my head which was bleeding freely   I got a pair of
scissors and cut off his hair and then began my first Job of
d[r]essing wounds upon examination I [found] the bear
had taken nearly all his head in his capcious mouth close
to his left eye on one side and clos to his right ear on the
other and laid the skull bare to near the crown of the head
leaving a white streak where his teeth passed   one of
his ears was torn from his head out to the outer rim   after
stitching all the other wounds in the best way I was capabl
and according to the captains directions the ear being the
last I told him I could do nothing for his Eare   O you
must try to stitch up some way or other said he   then
I put in my needle stitching it through and through and
over and over laying the lacerated parts togather as nice
as I could with my hands" *

After this Jed was able to mount his horse to travel back
to camp. Here a tent was pitched for him, and his wounds
were washed. Eventually he recovered, but he was badly
scarred for life. To conceal the horribly mangled ear and
other marks, he always wore his hair long.

* *James Clyman, American Frontiersman* 1792–1881, Charles L. Camp
(California Historical Society).

It was on this trip that Jed crossed South Pass, the historic gateway to the Oregon country. He was one of the first to make the passage, almost twenty years before the steady stream of emigration started on the Oregon Trail.

By the time that Jed returned to St. Louis in 1826, he was recognized as one of the leading men in the fur trade. A few months later he led a trapping expedition to California, which was then Mexican territory. To Americans it was an almost uncharted land. After crossing the Continental Divide on the way west, the trappers found themselves in a bleak wasteland where they suffered cruelly from hunger.

When they came to the land of the Mojave Indians in California, they did not know what to expect, for the Mojaves were fierce fighters. Yet the Indians were kind, feeding them well and taking good care of them.

After a pleasant stay of two weeks, they left with some Mojave guides and headed for the Pacific coast. On this stage of their journey the travelers found beautiful scenery, well-watered land, and large herds of cattle and horses. The friars of the Franciscan missions were just as hospitable as the Mojave Indians had been.

This visit of the trappers was the first meeting of two alien cultures in California. Smith's expedition, unimpressive as it was in the vastness of the region, was the forerunner of American penetration into California. The Mexican governor, oppressed by grim thoughts of the future influx of many more Americans, brusquely ordered Smith off California territory.

Jed obeyed the order to the extent of departing with some of his men, going back by a different route in order to learn more about the country. Passing through the San Joaquin Valley, the trappers saw herds of antelope and elk by the thousands, and flocks of birds so numerous that they shadowed the sun. On the way they trapped beaver successfully along the San Joaquin River.

On the return journey Jed took along two companions to find the best route east through the Great Salt Desert of Nevada and Utah. Soon they came to a forbidding seventy-five-mile stretch without water. The sun, reflected on the salt-encrusted surface of the desert, beat down on them pitilessly. Shimmering heat waves created appealing mirages, while salt-bearing winds threatened to choke them.

This is how Jed later described the critical day in his journal:

"With our best exertion we pushed forward walking as we had been for a long time over the soft sand. That kind of traveling is verry tiresome to men in good health who can eat when and what they choose and drink as often as they desire, and to us worn down with hunger and fatigue and burning with thirst increased by the blazing sands it was almost insurportable. At about 4 O Clock we were obliged to stop on the side of a sand hill under the shade of a small Cedar. We dug holes in the sand and laid down in them for the purpose of cooling our heated bodies. After resting about an hour we resumed our wearysome journey, and traveled until 10 O Clock at night, when we laid down to take a little repose. . . . Our sleep was not repose, for tormented nature made us dream of things we had not and for the want of which it then seemed possible and even probable we might perish in the desert unheard and unpitied. In those moments how trifling were all those things that hold such an absolute sway over the busy and prosperous world. My dreams were not of Gold or ambitious honors but of my distant quiet home, of murmuring brooks of Cooling Cascades. After a short rest we continued our march and traveled all night. The murmur of falling waters still sounding in our ears and the apprehension that we might never live to hear that sound in reality weighed heavily uppon us. . . ." *

The next morning their ordeal came to an end as they found water at last. Refreshed and rested, Jed and his companions continued on their way. The rest of their trip home was uneventful.

The following year Jed led another expedition headed for California. But this time he met with disaster at the hands of the Mojaves, who for some reason unknown to the white men had suddenly turned hostile. While the party was crossing the Colorado River on homemade rafts, the Indians attacked them savagely.

* *The Travels of Jedediah Smith*, Maurice S. Sullivan (Fine Arts Press).

When the slaughter was over, there were only a few survivors. All their horses and equipment were gone. They were left with five rifles, a little ammunition, and a few pounds of dried meat.

Grimly the trappers barricaded themselves in a cotton-wood grove, trying to make the best of their slim chance of holding out against hundreds of Mojaves. When the men asked Jed whether he thought they could hold out, he recorded that "I told them I thought we would," adding to himself that "that was not my opinion."

It was a desperate chance, but the excellent shooting of the mountain men discouraged the Indians. After several had been killed, the rest made off, allowing the trappers to escape.

But their troubles were far from over. It took them nine days to cross the Mojave Desert, with an unbearably hot sun pouring down upon them. There was no water, but they managed to extract a little moisture from cactus plants.

At last they reached the coastal plain, where they were again hospitably received at the Franciscan missions. By September, 1827, they were able to rejoin the main party that they had left in California the year before. There were new difficulties with the governor, who was dismayed to find that he had not seen the last of the Americans.

At last Jed was able to start the return trip with his men. But by then it was November, and snow and frost in the mountains made traveling difficult and hazardous. In fact the trappers made such painfully slow progress that their Indian guides lost heart and stole away.

What was to be done? Perhaps, Jed reasoned, they might do better to turn north and head for the Oregon country. It was an unfortunate decision—in one of those disagreeable situations where every choice seemed the wrong one. For the new mountain road appeared even more impenetrable than the earlier one had been.

But Jed and his men continued to head north under heartbreaking conditions. For a time, two miles a day was the best progress they could make. Nevertheless Jed did his best to hearten his men in the face of new hardships. One after another their animals perished. Soon they found themselves in hostile country, and constant marauding by the Indians added to their sufferings.

Still they persevered and continued north. Winter passed, and spring too, and by the end of June, 1828, they crossed the California-Oregon border. Now, after all their sufferings, when it seemed that the worst was over, came the cruelest blow of all. On July 14, all but four members of the party were massacred in an Indian attack.

Jed was one of the four survivors who managed to make their slow, painful way to the Hudson's Bay trading post at Fort Vancouver. Arriving in the last stages of exhaustion, they had completed an epic journey over a thousand miles of rugged wilderness terrain. It was a great feat, but such epics were common in the history of the mountain men.

John McLoughlin, who headed the post at Vancouver, received the Americans with his customary kindness and hospitality. They were his business rivals, and he would not have dreamed of lifting a finger to give them the slightest help in promoting their business affairs. But aside from that they were human beings, and sorely in need of all the rest and care they could get.

And so McLoughlin gladly played the genial and considerate host. Who would have thought, to see him together with his grateful guests, that at that very moment Americans and Englishmen were hotly disputing the ownership of the vast Oregon country?

After Jed and his men had completely recovered from the effects of the hardships they had endured, they made their way back to a rendezvous in the Rockies. From then on Jed continued to prosper. He was not only a first-rate trapper and leader, he was also a good businessman—a combination rare in the history of the fur trade.

Good trappers, as we have seen, gave little thought to money. And what prudent businessman would have wanted to put up with the dangers and privations of a trapper's life? When Jed Smith turned to the business end of the fur trade, he might have succeeded in living to a ripe old age if he had been prudent.

But instead of giving himself up wholeheartedly to business, Jed could not resist the lure of the West. While traveling with a caravan on the Santa Fe Trail, he left the main party to explore the country near the Cimarron River. There he was brutally murdered by a war band of Comanche Indians.

Jed Smith was only thirty-two at the time of his death. He was sincerely mourned by the mountain men, for there was no one quite like him. His crude fellow-trappers noted, with a kind of wonderment, that he was a mild man and a Christian. It was a minor miracle that "with his ears constantly filled with the language of the profane and the dissolute, no evil communication proceeded out of his mouth."

Even in the wilderness Jed went to the trouble of shaving regularly, instead of growing the customary unkempt beard. Not an important detail, perhaps, but it bespoke his inner discipline, his self-respect, and his sense of what a leader should be. Similarly, he avoided tobacco and strong drink, and never joined in the wild sprees that ended the trapping season.

Yet there was no indication that the mountain men thought of him as priggish. He was one of those rare men who are born leaders—gentle, innately considerate of his comrades, but also gallant, incisive, and readily obeyed. For all their fiercely independent spirit and their love of crude horseplay, the trappers freely acknowledged Jedediah Smith as their superior. And what greater compliment could a mountain man pay anyone?

8
JIM BRIDGER

To USE expressions like "the typical mountain man" would be a serious mistake. They were all individualists; indeed, they were truly rugged individualists. Each one was a law unto himself to an extent that was impossible for people who lived in a civilized community.

The three mountain men we have read about so far had more differences than points of similarity. John Colter was the forerunner, the almost legendary hero of the early days of Rocky Mountain trapping. Old Bill Williams was a saturnine curmudgeon, at odds with himself and everybody else. Jed Smith was the natural leader born to command men.

And what of Jim Bridger, who together with Kit Carson was to become the most famous of the mountain men?

Here is how David L. Brown, a contemporary, described Bridger:

"He was perfectly ignorant of all knowledge contained in books, not even knowing the letters of the alphabet; put perfect faith in dreams and omens, and was unutterably scandalized if even the most childish of the superstitions of the Indians were treated with anything like contempt or disrespect; for in all these he was a firm and devout believer."

And why not? Jim married an Indian girl; his children were half-Indian; the man who was perhaps his best friend was Washakie, the great chief of the Shoshone Indians. In fact, it is quite possible that Jim spent almost as much of his life in the company of Indians—friendly, hostile, and teetering somewhere in between—as he did with white people.

But the same observer pointed out other qualities: Jim was brave and resourceful, a hunter who could bring down twenty buffaloes with twenty consecutive shots, a leader who was nicknamed "Old Gabe" as a tribute to his skill and prudence.

Above all, Jim was credited with a photographic memory. Place him anywhere in the West from the Canadian border to the Rio Grande, and he knew how to proceed.

Whenever there was a dispute about how to reach a certain place or stream, whenever the other trappers were in doubt about the best course to follow, Jim Bridger was the final authority:

"He would throw his gun carelessly over his shoulder, survey the country awhile with his eye, and then strike out on a course, and never fail to reach the place, although he had several hundred miles to traverse over a country which he had never traveled, and to places he had never seen."

This combination of photographic memory of places once seen, coupled with his sure instinct for reaching places unknown, made Jim the great mountain man he was. He had a pictorial mind that no bookish man could have matched.

And there were many facets to Jim's skill. To know where a river flowed was not enough. He had to know where it was deep and where it was shallow, where the current was swift and where it was sluggish, where and when it could be navigated or crossed. To know where the mountain passes were—that was fine. But what months of the year were they open? How could they be reached in different seasons? Where were the good camp sites? How safe were they? How much forage for animals was nearby? Jim had to know the answers to these questions and hundreds of others.

Jim Bridger was born in Virginia in 1804, about the time that Lewis and Clark were starting out on their memorable journey of exploration to the Far West.

When Jim was eight years old his family moved to Missouri. Before he was fourteen both of his parents died. Without any schooling or training to speak of, he was left with the problem of supporting a younger sister.

For a while Jim ran a ferry across the Mississippi—tiring work that required great strength and considerable presence of mind. Then he became an apprentice to a blacksmith, which gave him an opportunity to pick up many useful skills. He learned how to fix wagon wheels, shoe horses, repair beaver traps, and make the large grappling hooks used by river boatmen.

But it was work without a future—or at least without a future that interested a youngster of Jim's lively temperament. Outside his door there was a constant procession of trappers, traders, Indians, army men, teamsters, muleteers, pioneers—all on their way west, to the glittering unknown.

Jim brooded and bided his time. At last, when he was eighteen, his great chance came: he joined the fur-trapping expedition headed by Colonel William H. Ashley and Major Andrew Henry. This party of about a hundred men was to sail up the Missouri to its source in the Rockies and then trap in the near-by country.

Most of the men were seasoned trappers, though there were some greenhorns like Jim and Jed Smith. Jim was hired mainly on the score of his physical strength and his ferrying and blacksmithing experience. The leaders of the expedition, who were necessarily keen judges of a man's potential abilities, rightly felt that what Jim did not know he would learn soon enough under the actual stress and danger of life in the wilderness.

The trip up the Missouri was, as always, slow and tortuous. Once arrived at their destination, the trappers met some Indians who were very friendly. The white men were relieved, so much so that they became careless. One night the "friendly" Indians staged a surprise raid and ran off every horse in the camp.

The trappers were stranded and helpless. The expedition could proceed no farther. The men built a fort, and then the group split up. Some of them would remain at the fort, while the rest returned home down the river, to come back the following spring with more trappers, more supplies, new animals. How much patience was required for such a trip!

From some friendly Indians and experienced trappers Jim learned how to treat buckskins, how to make his own moccasins and mend his clothes. Soon winter came on, with below-freezing temperatures and bitter, icy gales that lashed the fort. But the men were snug enough in their dwelling and rarely ventured out.

Finally, when March arrived, the three-foot layer of ice on the river began to break up with resounding crashes, smashing big trees as if they were made of paper. Jim was proud of himself, for a man who had spent a full winter in the mountains could consider himself a *hivernant* ("winterer"). Now he was a real trapper.

In the following months the party was involved in several skirmishes with hostile Indians. The prospect of further

fighting was troublesome. Not only were the trappers in constant danger, but they had little hope of profitable trapping in the presence of warlike Indians.

In August of that year (1823), after one of these Indian battles, there occurred an incident that was to prove a turning point in Jim's life. An old trapper named Hugh Glass went out hunting with two companions. As he walked into a small clearing he found himself almost face to face with a huge female grizzly and her two cubs.

He was hemmed in on all sides by thickets. The other two trappers, more favorably situated, made good their escape to camp. As the bear advanced ponderously toward him, Glass fired. It was a good shot, well and coolly aimed.

Eventually the shot would have proved fatal, but the immediate result was that the bear, with an appalling roar of rage, leaped on Glass with its three-inch claws and slashed his thigh and shoulder to the bone.

Meanwhile his companions reported his "death" and rounded up other trappers to search for the bear. When they caught up with the dying animal, they poured enough lead into her to finish her sufferings at once.

Glass, surprisingly enough, was still alive despite his terrible mauling. The trappers treated his wounds as best they could and carried him back carefully to camp. It was clear he could not survive much longer. He was bedded on robes and blankets and made as comfortable as was possible under the circumstances.

All night long the old man groaned and writhed in agony, yet when morning came he was still alive.

What was to be done? The trappers could not take him along with them, nor could they stay with him indefinitely. Neither could they desert him and leave him to his fate.

At last the leader had a suggestion. Let two men stay with Glass until his fate was decided; after he died, they could catch up with the rest of the group. Who would volunteer? As the leader's gaze rested on each trapper in turn, they turned aside shamefacedly, but no one offered to stay.

If the trappers had been story-book heroes or the glamorous figures that legend has made familiar, they would have stayed. But, ringed about as they were by hostile Indians, they realized that anyone who agreed to remain might be signing his own death warrant. For months they had been under a constant strain as they awaited an Indian attack at any moment.

Unnerved as they were, the trappers found ready reasons for their callous attitude. And yet their consciences troubled them. Finally they raised a purse of eighty dollars to pay any two members of the group who would be willing to care for the dying man until his sufferings were over. After more uncomfortable palavering, two volunteers reluctantly stepped forth.

One of these trappers was an experienced veteran named Fitzgerald. The other volunteer was one of the youngest members of the expedition, who remains unnamed in the earlier versions of this incident.

While the main party of trappers went on their way, the two uneasy volunteers remained with Glass. They tended his wounds, changed the dressings, and did what they could to make him comfortable. Forty-eight hours went by and the old man was still alive, despite his loss of blood.

With every moment that passed the volunteers became more uneasy. The slightest sound startled them. They were afraid to shoot any game or light a fire because they might betray their whereabouts to prowling Indians.

On the third day they saw definite indications that Indians were near them. Fitzgerald was in a panic of fear.

He wanted to run away while there was still time to be saved. But what was to be done with the old man who stubbornly lingered on?

Fitzgerald kept nagging his companion to run away with him. At last the impressionable boy could hold out no longer. They would rejoin the main party with the story that the old man had died. And, to bear out their tale, they would bring back his belongings—his rifle, powder horn, knife, and flint. After all, he was on the verge of dying. It was an ugly end to this story of human weakness.

After the two trappers had rejoined the main party, several months passed busily in hunting and trapping. The attack on Hugh Glass had taken its place with all those incidents that formed the pattern of a trapper's daily life.

And yet the story was to have a fantastic epilogue. One night, as the younger of the two deserters came back to camp after a day's hunting, he was horrified to see a scrawny figure with blazing eyes loom up before him in the firelight. Was it a ghost, or was it Hugh Glass?

It was the old man—alive! He had not died after all, and he had an amazing story to tell. After being left all alone, he had given way to rage as he thought of his plight —left helpless to face starvation and death.

Soon unbearable thirst goaded the wounded old man to crawl agonizingly to a near-by stream. After drinking, he was so spent that he lay on the bank for several days.

The old man had amazing powers of endurance. After

his enforced rest, he was able to crawl toward the Missouri, progressing about two miles a day and living on roots and berries. His thigh wound improved steadily, as he was able to wash it. But his shoulder wound, which he could not reach, was in a "terrible condition."

For forty days Glass continued his wearisome advance, until one day he was discovered by a band of Sioux Indians. The savages, more kindly than his white companions, took pity on him and tended his wounds carefully. After a while they brought him to a small trading post where he could be tended by his own people.

The old man remained at the post for two months. His wounds gradually healed, but he was so emaciated that he looked like little more than a skeleton. His new friends gave him a complete outfit of clothes, a rifle, a butcher knife, and all the other paraphernalia of a trapper.

Despite his sufferings, Glass was anxious to rejoin the trappers who had wronged him so cruelly. And so, when he learned that his friends were taking a boat up the Missouri, he went with them. But ill luck still pursued him. The party was ambushed by a band of Arikaras. Glass was the only one to escape to safety. Once more he was on his own.

After a few days of wandering he staggered into a village of the friendly Mandan Indians, where he recuperated his strength. Once more he set out for the camp of Major Henry's trappers. He had hundreds of miles to cover, most of the distance over the country of the Blackfeet, those

implacable enemies of the white man. At one point he was
held up for two days by a huge herd of buffalo crossing a
shallow stretch of the Missouri.

At last, when he was so weary that he was seriously thinking of returning to the Mandan village to spend the winter,
he encountered the trappers he had been seeking on his
long trek. Yet his meeting with the young man who had
deserted him was different from what he had pictured. When
he saw the shame and remorse and relief pictured on the
youngster's face, his anger melted and he forgave him.

The story of Hugh Glass's miraculous recovery became
one of the enduring epics of the mountain men, told and
retold time and again. But what particularly interests us
is that most modern authorities believe that the young man

who deserted him was Jim Bridger. They believe, too, that the incident had a lifelong influence on him. From then on, he was determined to be his own master and make his own decisions. No longer would he be influenced or led by other men.

Whether or not the accusation was justified, it is unquestionable that from then on Jim Bridger was noted for his deep sense of responsibility and his upright and generous dealings with his fellow-trappers. No mountain man had a better reputation for being reliable and dependable.

It took very little time for Jim Bridger to become one of the best trappers in the business. Long before he was thirty he was one of the outstanding leaders of trapping expeditions. He was unequaled as an explorer, and he knew how to deal with the Indians. Even at that early age he was affectionately known among the trappers as "Old Gabe."

Jim was over six feet tall and muscular—without an ounce of superfluous flesh. "He might have served as a model for a sculptor or painter," wrote one man who met him in those days, "by which to express the perfection of graceful strength and easy activity. . . . His cheek bones were high, his nose hooked, the expression of his eye mild and thoughtful, and that of his face grave almost to solemnity."

The serious expression could be deceptive, for Jim Bridger was to become the most expert of the mountain men in relating wildly fantastic stories without the slightest change of expression.

At least in his youthful days, Jim was involved in as many Indian fights as Kit Carson. But whereas Carson depended on split-second timing to escape alive, Jim sometimes overawed the Indians by sheer force of character. He also relied often on his friendship with the Shoshone Indians.

In actual fighting, Jim was inimitably crafty, and often outwitted the savages by some trick that was as sly as it was completely unexpected. But he also had a reputation for fair dealing that even the Blackfeet, the white man's worst enemies, could rely on.

Once when a Blackfoot and his wife and daughter blundered into Jim Bridger's camp by mistake, his trappers, smarting from a particularly severe struggle with the Blackfeet, wanted to kill the unfortunate Indians out of hand. But Bridger protected the savages, ordered his men not to touch them, and accompanied them to safety. As the grateful Indians left him, the women raised their hands, palms out, in the gesture of benediction. Such incidents were memorable in a region where men were so often exposed to death that they readily formed the habit of shooting first and investigating later.

During the 1830's the fur trade was steadily petering out, and Jim realized that he had to find some other way to make a living. He hit on an excellent idea: to build a trading post on the Oregon Trail.

How this famous route came into being makes an interesting story. For decades trappers and traders had passed back and forth between St. Louis and the Oregon country. In the course of their journeys they discovered the best trails and crossings on the way.

Strictly speaking, the "discoveries" of the white man were actually rediscoveries: they were merely using the paths and trails that had been used from much earlier times by the Indians. Long ago the natives had found the routes that offered the fewest obstacles to travel. Naturally, those routes were destined to become the most popular ones. In time they made up the Oregon Trail, two thousand miles long.

To us, accustomed to the magnificent automobile highways of our own day, the Oregon Trail has one curious feature: *none of it was man-made*. The roadbed and the grades were as nature had left them. There were no bridges or tunnels or other aids to travel. The Rockies seemed an insurmountable obstacle for wagon trains until Frémont's explorations in 1842 publicized the existence of South Pass.

Emigrants took the Oregon Trail from Westport Landing (now Kansas City) in Missouri. After covering some 660 miles through Kansas and Nebraska, they reached the first great stopping place—Fort Laramie, at the junction of the North Platte and Laramie Rivers in southeastern Wyoming.

If the pioneers were wise enough to start out in late spring, they had ample grass for their animals. The springtime floods were over, the Trail was in fine condition for travel, the region was rich in game, and the streams were comparatively easy to ford.

For those who started out later, traveling on the Oregon Trail was full of hardship. The prairies were parched, and the weary emigrants were buried in clouds of dust. The streams were dried up, and humans and animals suffered cruelly from thirst as the midsummer sun poured down fiercely on them. Draft animals were exhausted, household goods were tossed aside to lighten the wagons. The skeletons of oxen, horses, and mules littered the Trail, and many a fresh-dug grave testified to the hardship and misery that had proved too much for some of the pioneers.

From Fort Laramie the route circled around the northern end of the Laramie Mountains in Wyoming. After another 170 miles the emigrants reached Independence Rock, a huge oval-shaped outcrop of some twenty-seven acres at the beginning of the valley of the Sweetwater River. (Before reaching this point, the weary travelers passed through many miles of territory where the water was too alkaline to be fit for drinking. The delightfully pure, fresh water of the Sweetwater accounts for the name of that river.)

Another hundred miles across Wyoming brought the emigrants across the Rockies through South Pass. They had now completed about half of their two-thousand-mile journey. Now veering in a southwesterly direction, the Trail proceeded another 120 miles to Fort Bridger in the southwestern corner of Wyoming.

The emigrants were ignorant of frontier ways. They were thoroughly worn out by the time they had crossed the

Rockies. Supplies were short, their animals were spent, some of their equipment had become worthless.

So Jim Bridger had an inspiration: why not build a fort and trading post where the pioneers could rest and repair and replenish their equipment? The site he picked was in the valley of a mountain stream which supplied precious water and was well stocked with trout.

Fort Bridger had other attractions. Its owner could give the weary emigrants a wealth of useful advice. He could protect them from the Indians, guide them on their way, sell them new equipment, or repair what was out of order. Here his old blacksmith training would prove useful! The fort was located on a river, with a toll ferry that proved quite profitable. Even the ferryman training of his boyhood came in handy.

Fort Bridger was actually astride two trails. The Oregon Trail proper led northwest for another nine hundred miles. To the southwest, the Overland Trail went on to Salt Lake Valley and from there to California. Still another advantage was that the fort was located in the territory of Jim's good friends, the Shoshone Indians. Thanks to his influence with the tribe, the emigrants passing through their country would suffer no harm from the Shoshones.

From the very beginning the fort prospered. It was a great meeting place for emigrants, traders, and friendly Indians. Jim was sociable and generous. He made plenty of money, and gave it away just as readily. He was well liked.

His information was reliable, his promises faithfully kept.

The old West, the trapper's paradise that Jim had once known and loved, was changing rapidly now. Settlers were pouring in by the thousands, and here and there the wilderness was slowly giving way to farms and straggling towns. Army posts were being extended farther west, territorial governments were bringing judges, juries, and jails to an area where every man had once been a law unto himself.

Jim Bridger had become something of an institution in the new West. Army officers and officials made a point of meeting him, and many of them left interesting descriptions of the encounters. In 1852, for example, G. B. Ferris, the newly appointed Secretary of Utah Territory, visited Fort Bridger with his wife. At that time Jim was forty-eight years old, and his trapping days had long been over. Mrs. Ferris left this vivid description of Jim and his surroundings:

"We encamped at Fort Bridger—a long, low, strongly

constructed log building, surrounded by a high wall of logs, stuck endwise in the ground. Bridger came out and invited us in, and introduced us to his Indian wife, and showed us his half-breed children—keen, bright-eyed little things.

"Everything was rude and primitive. This man strongly attracted my attention; there was more than civility about him—there was native politeness. He is the oldest trapper in the Rocky Mountains; his language is very graphic and descriptive, and he is evidently a man of great shrewdness."

Not the least of Jim's social graces was his ability to spin tall tales. All the mountain men were masters of this art, which was their substitute for reading and going to the theater; but Jim Bridger was universally acknowledged as the leading teller of tall tales.

Like John Colter, he told many a true story of the wonders of Yellowstone that was taken for imaginative yarn-spinning. But unlike Colter, Jim ironically added many fanciful details to the facts. Since he wasn't believed, he decided that he might as well build up the stories in any fashion that his roaming imagination dictated.

In trappers' lore the fantastic Petrified Forest of Arizona met the same fate as the geological exaggerations of Yellowstone. The scientists tell us that 160,000,000 years ago the trees died in an Arizona forest and a stream carried them off to a near-by shallow sea that has long since vanished. As the dead trees floated along, the bark, branches, and most of the roots fell off; what was left sank to the bottom.

Volcanic eruptions in this region covered the wood with layers of ash and thus preserved it against rotting. Meanwhile the silica in the ash dissolved in the water and penetrated the wood so thoroughly that it was turned into various forms of quartz: carnelian, opal, jasper, onyx, agate. The variety of beautiful colors became even more striking when other minerals, such as iron and manganese, were carried in by the stream and mingled with the petrified matter.

The layers of petrified forests in Yellowstone are in their way just as remarkable. There too one may see trees that have been turned into stone. In one area the Lamar River has eroded a spectacular cliffside and thus uncovered two thousand feet of alternating layers of petrified trees and volcanic ash.

This stunning sight was undoubtedly well known to Jim. So when other trappers told him about the Petrified Forest of Arizona he was not too astonished. The story is told that one night at a gathering of trappers, one of them was describing his travels in the Southwest.

"Ever been down thar, Jim?"

"No, why should I—no beaver thar."

"But there are other things thar—last winter I saw huge trees all turned to stone."

"Oh," said Jim, sensing a tall tale that needed to be topped, "that's peetrification. Come to the Yellowstone with me and I'll show you real peetrification: peetrified trees still a-growin', with peetrified birds on 'em a-singin' peetrified songs!"

For several years the Mormons in Utah had been jealous of Jim's prosperity at Fort Bridger. They felt that the popularity of his post deflected a lot of valuable trading from their own communities. Eventually their hostility reached such a point that they invaded Jim's territory in 1853 and seized the fort. Four years later, when the United States Army was in control, it took over Fort Bridger and held it on lease from Jim. The fort remained an army post until 1890.

In the 1850's Jim spent more and more of his time as a guide for United States Army expeditions. In a land where strangers could become hopelessly lost, where Indians were still a constant danger, and where water was scarce, Jim's talents as a guide were invaluable.

Repeatedly the officers were astounded at Jim's photographic memory. Thus Captain Humfreville, who knew him well, wrote admiringly:

"Although Bridger had little or no education, he could, with a piece of charcoal or a stick, scratch on the ground or any smooth surface a map of the whole western country that was much more correct than those made at that time by skilled topographical engineers, with all their scientific instruments. I have seen Bridger look at a printed map, and point out its defects at sight."

Jim's services were much in demand on expeditions

against the Indians and in road surveys. On one of his
assignments he laid out a course from Fort Bridger to the
South Platte River, hundreds of miles away. This trail had
so many advantages that it was later used by the Pony Express, the Overland Stage, and finally the Union Pacific
Railroad.

In his old age Jim became interested in literature. When
Captain Humfreville showed him a copy of *Hiawatha*, the
old man was fascinated. He might not know anything about
literature, but after all the poem was about Indians, and
who knew more about Indians than Jim Bridger did? So
Jim, who could not read, begged the Captain to read him
the story of Hiawatha. What happened then greatly
amused the Captain.

"He would sit bent over, his long legs crossed, his gaunt
hands and arms clasping his knees, and listen to the reading
attentively, until a passage was reached in which Long-
fellow portrayed an imaginary Indian, when Bridger, after
a period of uneasy wriggling on his seat, arose very wrathy
and swearing that the whole story was a lie, that he would
listen to no more of it, and that 'no such Injun ever lived.'

"This happened over and over again. After a while I
quieted him and began reading again, but after a short
time he was sure to stop me, swearing that he would not
listen any longer to such infernal lies."

At length Jim wanted to know what was the best book
written in the language. Captain Humfreville told him

that Shakespeare's plays were generally conceded to be the finest work written in English.

So Jim "made a journey to the main road and lay in wait for a wagon train and sought a copy from some emigrants, paying for it with a yoke of cattle, which at that time could have been sold for $125. He hired a German boy from one of the wagon trains at $40 a month to read to him."

Luckily the youngster was an excellent reader, and Jim was so interested that he listened to the reading for hours at a stretch. "Occasionally he got the thread of the story so mixed that he would swear a blue streak, then compel the young man to stop, turn back, and re-read a page or two, until he could get the story straightened out.

"After that it was amusing to hear Bridger quote Shakespeare. He could give quotation after quotation, and was always ready to do so. Sometimes he seasoned them with a broad oath, so ingeniously inserted as to make it appear to the listener that Shakespeare himself had used the same language."

Jim liked the army officers, and they liked him and respected his masterly judgment. Yet they listened to his stories about the Yellowstone region with a grain of salt, calling them "old Jim Bridger's lies."

In his sixties he was still a striking figure, "straight as an Indian, muscular and quick in movement, but not nervous or excitable; in weight probably 160 pounds; with an eye piercing as the eye of an eagle, that seemed to flash fire when narrating an experience that had called out his reserve power. There was nothing in his costume or deportment to indicate the heroic spirit that dwelled within, simply a plain, unassuming man."

In 1865 Jim Bridger became Chief of Scouts for the United States Army. But by now his career was approaching its end. Jim had become a legend during his own lifetime. Young officers fresh from West Point were too cocksure to accept the advice of this aging man who had passed his prime a long time ago.

At first Jim was exasperated, then cantankerous. But he knew the time had come to make way for younger men. In 1868, at the age of sixty-four, he retired.

Jim's last thirteen years were spent in peaceful retirement. His vision got worse and worse until toward the end he went blind. He loved to tell stories of the great days to his children and grandchildren, who hung on his words. Old and tired as Jim Bridger was, he often became restless because all his life he had worked hard and been a man of action.

What a pity it is that during those thirteen peaceful years no writer came to see him to get the story of his life from his own lips! So all that is left today to remind us of Jim Bridger is part of the original structure of his fort, now preserved in Fort Bridger National Park. But that is not quite all, for much of the Far West today is a monument to Jim Bridger.

9 KIT CARSON

ALONG WITH Daniel Boone, Davy Crockett, and Buffalo Bill, Kit Carson is one of the great folk heroes of the American frontier. To look the part, Kit should have been a tall, powerfully built man exuding self-confidence. Actually he was below middle height, tow headed, blue eyed, bandy legged, quiet spoken and mild mannered; not at all an impressive-looking man.

What then made Kit the great frontiersman he truly was? He had a quality that few people possess. When a crisis came up, when life and death hung in the balance, he perceived the danger at once. But instead of becoming paralyzed with fright, he saw with lightning speed what had to be done.

If there was only one chance to escape—no matter how desperately slight—he found it, took it, and came through successfully. For years he lived in constant danger, yet he lived to a goodly age and died in bed.

Christopher Carson was born in Kentucky on December 25, 1809. He was one of fourteen children. When Kit was still an infant, his father took the family west to Franklin, Missouri. This was, in fact, America's westernmost settlement at the time, founded by old Dan'l Boone when he felt that Kentucky was getting too crowded.

Eight hundred miles southwest of Franklin was the town of Santa Fe in New Mexico. Settled by the Spaniards about 1605, Santa Fe is the second oldest city in what is now United States territory. From time to time occasional parties of American trappers and traders came to Santa Fe to do business. The Spaniards treated them harshly, and only generous bribes staved off imprisonment and confiscation of the trade goods.

But in the years that Kit was growing up, the Mexicans revolted against Spanish rule and gained their freedom. The merchants of Santa Fe were eager to obtain a variety of American goods. In return they offered beautifully woven blankets, handsome Mexican saddles, combs, intricately fashioned jewelry, and best of all, an ample supply of Mexican silver dollars with a good, clear ring. (Mexican dollars were so highly prized on the American frontier that they were American legal tender until 1857!)

In 1821 the first American wagon train loaded with trade

goods set out from Franklin along the Santa Fe Trail. The famous trail passed through country that was inhabited only for the last fifty miles. Most of the trip was over the prairie, and some went over a barren desert where there was often acute suffering from lack of water.

The greatest drawback of the trail, however, was that it was infested by some of the fiercest Plains Indians, particularly the Comanches. Traveling in a large group was comparatively safe, hence the American traders made a point of going to Santa Fe in fairly large caravans.

Such a wagon train enlisted all sorts and conditions of men. There were the traders, intent on a handsome profit. The burly teamsters, uncouth in appearance and profane in the most casual phrase, were particularly attractive figures to a youngster like Kit. So were the Mexican *vaqueros*, in their outlandish conical hats and glamorous clothes with silver trimmings. All these people were familiar figures in Franklin.

Poor Kit was unhappy. He was so short that he was often contemptuously dismissed as a "runt." His father had died, and his stepfather had apprenticed him to a saddler. But Kit, who was almost sixteen, hated the work.

It was all drudgery to him—and doubly so when the mountain men and Conestoga wagon drivers swaggered into the saddlery and in their idle moments told stories of their adventures that fired the unhappy boy's lively imagination. That he was a runt made him all the more eager to play a man's part and share in the frontiersmen's glory.

The Indians, the desert, the broiling sun—these dangers and miseries meant nothing to him. The frontiersmen were their own masters, for better or worse. It was a matter of free choice. Drudgery that was imposed by a master was unbearable. But drudgery that you endured willingly was easy to bear; you were buoyed up by a thrilling sense of freedom.

By the time that Kit was nearly seventeen, he had served two years of his apprenticeship. He still had five years to go. Every day his work became more intolerable.

Finally Kit could stand it no longer. He ran away to join a wagon train that was on its way to Santa Fe.

His master was apparently not too grieved at his sudden departure, for he placed this advertisement with its humorous ending in a Missouri newspaper:

NOTICE: TO WHOM IT MAY CONCERN: That Christopher Carson, a boy about sixteen years old, small for his age, but thickset, light hair, ran away from the subscriber, living in Franklin, Howard County, Mo., to whom he had been bound to learn the saddler's trade, on or about the first day of September. He is supposed to have made his way to the upper part of the State. All persons are notified not to harbor, support, or subsist said boy under penalty of the law. One cent reward will be given to any person who will bring back the said boy.

DAVID WORKMAN

From the conversations Kit had heard he knew in a general way the routine of a wagon-train trip. Fifteen miles a day was considered a fair rate of speed. Since water was not always available, a creek or a spring made a convenient camping site. The animals were loosed and placed in a corral formed by a circular arrangement of the wagons. Guards were posted throughout the night to be on the lookout against Indian attack.

In the morning the camp was all bustle and confusion, which eventually turned into order. The biggest job was getting harnesses and saddles on the animals and fastening them to the wagons. Sometimes the wagon train moved in single file, almost a mile long. Other times—and this was the safer arrangement—the caravan advanced in three or four compact, parallel lines. The shouts of the drivers and the outriders, the creaking of the wagon wheels, the loud cracking of the bull whips, and the jolly chatter of the whole party created a cheerful atmosphere that lifted everyone's spirits.

Kit's job was to take care of the *caballada*—the loose animals. There were over a hundred of these—extra mules, lame oxen, mares with their foals, saddle horses, beef cattle. It was not easy to keep them together, especially when thirst made them restless. At night there was always the danger that wolves might attack the animals or that Indians would attempt to run some of them off.

But Kit, young as he was, was good at the job and learned

quickly. He became the hero of the expedition when he helped amputate the arm of an unfortunate man who had been wounded and was threatened with gangrene. Of course Kit had no theoretical knowledge of surgery, but he had seen such operations performed in Franklin and relied on his memory. The seasoned frontiersmen looked on approvingly when they saw how competently the youngster took on a dreadful responsibility that would have dazed many a mature man.

After the expedition arrived at its destination in Santa Fe and everyone was paid off, Kit went on to Taos to meet the trappers who came there to sell their furs. There he learned many tricks of the trade by listening to the trappers' tales.

When the trappers were away in the wilderness, Kit would take odd jobs, always learning new skills and adding to his photographic memory of lonely trails and imperceptible landmarks. He thoroughly enjoyed his stay in Taos, which was a fascinating place, with its Mexican merchants, its easygoing artisans, its dark-eyed Mexican girls, and Indians from the plains, pueblos, and mountains, as well as occasional American trappers, traders, and smugglers.

Because of his youth and short stature, it was not easy for Kit to be accepted by the rough mountain men. However, before he was twenty he took part in a trapping expedition that left Taos for California. This was in 1829; like Jed Smith, Kit was one of the earliest Americans to travel extensively in California. At an early age he covered thousands of miles in the Southwest, acquiring a knowledge of the country that he put to good use later on when he was a guide for Frémont's expeditions and a scout for the American Army.

On his first trip, despite his youth and inexperience, Kit distinguished himself in fighting off raids by the treacherous and bloodthirsty Apaches. Because of their unfamiliarity with the travel routes to California, the trappers chose the worst possible way—through the Mojave Desert.

The men suffered almost to the limit of their endurance. For, like Jed Smith's party, they were wracked by starvation and thirst and plagued by fierce sandstorms.

It was a cruel test for a youngster, but Kit handled himself so well that he earned the respect of the most experienced mountain men. At last, after taking refuge in a Spanish mission, the weary men rested up and then set out on a four-hundred-mile trapping expedition.

During this trip they stopped at another mission, where they were asked to recapture some runaway Indians who had stolen off to join a hostile tribe. Finding the fugitive Indians in the wilderness seemed a hopeless assignment, but despite his youth Kit was put in charge of a small band to round up the runaways.

Eventually Kit trailed them to a fairly large Indian village. Untroubled by the fact that his little force was greatly outnumbered, Kit stationed his men to such good advantage that his surprise attack overwhelmed a much larger Indian force. After some sharp fighting he was able to bring back the runaways, who were identified by his Indian guides.

Later on, when an Indian raid resulted in the theft of sixty horses, Kit was assigned to recover the stolen animals. His skillful tracking finally located the marauders. After routing them with a surprise attack at dawn, he recovered over fifty horses. These two exploits established Kit as one of the leading mountain men.

But these incidents, exciting as they were, were only incidental to the main objective of the expedition: trapping beaver. By the time the season was over, the trappers had peltries worth $24,000. If they returned to Taos with the furs, the Mexican government would very likely confiscate the pelts. The trappers would have nothing—not even a good time—to show for all the hardships they endured.

Kit had displayed his courage and determination in fighting. Now he showed that he could be resourceful when it came to the problems of peaceful activity. At his suggestion the furs were cached in an abandoned copper mine. Then Ewing Young, head of the expedition, "innocently" went to Santa Fe and obtained a permit from the Mexican governor of New Mexico for trading with the Indians.

At that point the mountain men left Santa Fe, creating the impression that they would do more trapping. Picking up the furs left at the copper mine, they returned to Santa Fe and sold the pelts.

The Mexicans were astonished at the apparent speed with which the Americans had obtained so many pelts. But the whole transaction was legal if not aboveboard, and there was nothing the indignant governor could do about it. Kit's plan had worked perfectly.

In the years that followed, Kit trapped beaver in many parts of the Rocky Mountain country. Quick thinking saved him repeatedly in his numerous scrapes with hostile Indians. Still, Kit was not boastful. Whenever people puffed up his exploits, he would merely comment mildly that their praises were "a leetle too thick."

Once, during a bitter skirmish with the Blackfeet Indians in Montana, Kit was shot in the shoulder. The wound bled profusely. Desperately Kit's comrades tried to stop the bleeding by stanching the wound with beaver fur—a standard trappers' remedy—but to no avail.

As night came on, Kit was delirious and suffering intensely from the cold. Weakened as he was, it did not seem that he would live until morning. But the cold weather saved him. For the sub-zero cold froze the dripping blood and thus closed the wound. Later he was skillfully treated by a squaw from a friendly tribe until he was fully recovered.

In that same year, 1834, Kit was hunting elk when he had the most terrifying of all his dangerous encounters with grizzly bears. It happened in the Medicine Bow Mountains, the outlying eastern range of the Rockies that extends through Colorado and Wyoming.

The sound of Kit's rifle roused two enormous grizzlies who were hidden in a thicket. As they came in sight they were about fifteen yards away from him, jaws open and claws extended for the kill. He did not have time to shoot, and there was no comrade present to save him.

Always acting quickly in emergencies, Kit made a dash for a grove of aspen trees. Picking out the one that had the broadest trunk, he seized a bough and swung himself up barely high enough to be out of the reach of the male's vicious claws.

The bough bent so far that Kit was afraid that it would break and bring him within range of the furious animals. A savage swipe of a paw ripped off one of his moccasins.

The male bear tried to reach him. Kit broke off a branch and smacked him hard on the snout. Roaring with pain, the grizzly took the delicate tree in its paws and bent it back and forth, trying to break it off. But, for all its apparent frailness, the aspen held firm.

Finally, just as it seemed that the grizzly might be making real progress, he noticed the presence of elk in the vicinity and made off in search of what seemed easier prey. It was the narrowest of Kit's many narrow escapes.

The following year Kit married a beautiful Arapaho girl named Waa-nibe. He won her hand only after a gun duel with a bullying French-Canadian trapper named Shunar. A giant of a man well over six feet tall, Shunar had terrorized the other mountain men. None of them dared pro-

test when he grabbed Waa-nibe roughly and insulted her.
The proud Arapahoes were goaded to threats of revenge,
and it looked as if a murderous free-for-all would break out.

Kit, despite his small stature, was the only mountain man
who was not afraid of Shunar. When the bully sneered in-
sultingly at him, Kit challenged him to a duel with pistols.
Then, in a fight to the death that reminds us of the Biblical

story of David and Goliath, Kit killed his formidable opponent. As a result, the grateful Arapaho chief presented his daughter in marriage to Kit.

The union was a happy one, but Kit was called away on so many assignments that he never achieved his ambition of putting an end to roving and living peacefully at home. A little girl was born to the Carsons, but after some years Waa-nibe sickened and died. Sorrowfully Kit sent his little daughter to St. Louis to be brought up in a convent.

It took Kit only a few years to assemble a choice group of first-rate mountain men, who were known as Carson's Men. By 1838 it was clear that the beaver fur trade was nearing its end. Kit had to find some other way to make a living.

He therefore became a buffalo hunter to supply meat to Bent's Fort, a famous trading post located in what is now southeastern Colorado. And, as more and more pioneers began to move west, Kit and his men had ready employment guarding the wagon trains.

It was dangerous work, for the Plains Indians were deeply resentful. The steady disappearance of the buffalo was gradually depriving them of their chief source of food; the steady encroachment of the white man was relentlessly stripping them of their land. The Indians fought back whenever an opportunity offered. So, as far as Kit was concerned, risking his life was merely part of the daily routine.

In 1842 Kit began a connection with the regular army that was to last intermittently for the rest of his life. That year a dashing young officer, Lieutenant John Charles Frémont, was assigned by the War Department to map out a convenient route that could be used by pioneers who intended to settle in the West.

Frémont owed his appointment to the efforts of his colorful and rambunctious father-in-law, Senator Thomas Hart Benton of Missouri, a staunch believer in westward expansion. The idea of establishing a favorable route was a sensible one, as it was bound to stimulate westward migration enormously.

It speaks well for Kit Carson that he was selected to guide this expedition, which had the avowed purpose of finding the best route to the Pacific. Frémont had deep admiration for Kit and trusted him implictly even on the most dangerous terrain. "With me," said Frémont, "Carson and Truth mean the same thing."

Another regular army officer, Lieutenant George Douglas Brewerton, who had many opportunities to observe Kit's work as a guide, left this fascinating portrait of him:

"A braver man than Kit perhaps never lived. In fact, I doubt if he ever knew what fear was. But with all this he exercised great caution. While arranging his bed, his saddle, which he always used as a pillow, was disposed in such a manner as to form a barricade for his head. His pistols, half-cocked, were placed above it, and his trusty rifle reposed beneath the blanket by his side, where it was not only ready for instant use, but perfectly protected from the damp. Except now and then to light his pipe, you never caught Kit at night exposing himself to the full glare of the camp-fire."

On that first expedition Kit took Frémont's men as far as South Pass (described on page 12), that all-important gateway to the western slopes of the Rockies. Thanks to the publicity that this trip received, Frémont became a popular hero. Forever after he was called "The Pathfinder."

Up to this time South Pass had been known only to mountain men like Jed Smith, Jim Bridger, and Kit. Now the route through the Pass became public knowledge. In 1843 the first great stream of emigrants started along the Oregon Trail, relying on South Pass to get them safely across the formidable barrier of the Rockies.

Frémont's second expedition, which set out in 1843, reached California after many hardships. In his account of the trip, the leader generously admitted more than once that without Kit to guide them, all the members of the expedition would have perished.

The third Frémont expedition which set out from Colorado in August, 1845, apparently had the objective of seizing California from the Mexicans. Kit set a course so well planned that it is still used today as an automobile road. After crossing the Rockies the explorers came to the salt flats west of Great Salt Lake. After that they found themselves in the Great Basin. This wasteland was over three hundred miles wide, but Kit was so well prepared for it that the crossing to California took two months less than any previous trip over the same route. Once in California, Kit played an important part in helping to secure California from Mexico for the United States in the "Bear Flag" Revolt.

In 1843 Kit had remarried. His bride was a beautiful Mexican girl, Josefa Jaramillo. When the Mexican War was over, Kit decided that it was time for him to settle down and devote himself to some profitable activity.

So for five years he raised cattle and horses on a New Mexico ranch. But it was a hard life, for there were continual skirmishes with horse-stealing Indians.

After that Kit took up dealing in sheep. He bought 6500 of the animals in California, drove them north to the Oregon Trail, and then brought them East, where he sold them for an excellent profit. He was now financially independent for the first time in his life.

But late in 1853 Kit was appointed United States Indian Agent at Taos. For a man of his strong sense of justice and incorruptible honesty, the job promised many worries, continual exasperation, irritating delays, countless war scares, and daily struggles with unscrupulous white men who took advantage of the Indians.

A less conscientious man would have turned down the offer. Kit of course accepted it. Though he had spent thirty years fighting Indians, he took his duties seriously and fought as hard as he knew how for the rights of his former enemies.

For example, Kit opposed the sale of liquor to the Indians and did his best to save their lands from seizure by the settlers who were pouring into the West. During his years of service as an Indian agent, the Utes and Apaches in his district remained at peace with the white man. They were impressed by his strict and evenhanded justice.

On the outbreak of the Civil War, however, many Indian tribes felt that their chance for revenge had come. As United States troops were withdrawn from the Southwest, the Apaches, Navahos, and Comanches carried out raids in the region, plundering and murdering the settlers.

Kit was no longer a young man, but he never dodged a crisis. After helping to organize the First New Mexico Volunteers, he commanded this force in a series of masterly campaigns that brought the Indians back to peaceful ways. When the war was over, Kit was promoted to the rank of brigadier general and placed in command of Fort Garland, Colorado, but he resigned this post in 1867 to resume his work as Indian agent. He died in 1868.

Kit Carson's rise from saddler's apprentice to brigadier general spanned a whole epoch in the history of the West. When Kit ran away to join the Santa Fe caravan, Missouri was still on the very tip of the frontier, the Indian still lorded it over thousands of unexplored square miles, and the fur trade was just about to experience the days of its greatest glory.

By the time of Kit's death, the United States stretched from "sea to shining sea." The doom of the Indian was clear to all. The trade in beaver fur had long been a thing of the past. The few mountain men still left were living on their memories. A bloody war had nearly ripped the nation in two, and it would take a long time to bind up the wounds. Meanwhile the first transcontinental railroad, symbol of the vanishing frontier, was nearing completion.

A new age was coming, and the mountain men had helped to usher in that new age. Kit Carson was barely able to read and write, yet as a trapper, Indian fighter, guide, scout, and military leader he made an unforgettable name for himself in the history of the West. For, together with the other mountain men, he was in the vanguard that made it possible for the pioneers to come to the West, to build their homes and farms and towns there, and to live peacefully under the law of the land.

BIBLIOGRAPHY

J. Cecil Alter, *Jim Bridger*. Salt Lake City: Shepard Book Company, 1925.

Charles L. Camp (Ed.), *James Clyman, American Frontiersman 1792–1881*. San Francisco: California Historical Society, 1928.

Hiram M. Chittenden, *A History of the American Fur Trade of the American Far West*. Stanford, Calif.: Academic Reprints, 1954.

Robert G. Cleland, *This Reckless Breed of Men*. New York: Alfred A. Knopf, Inc., 1950.

Philip St. George Cooke, *Scenes and Adventures in the Army*. Philadelphia: Lindsay & Blakiston, 1859.

Bernard De Voto, *Across the Wide Missouri*. Boston: Houghton Mifflin Company, 1947.

Bernard De Voto, *The Course of Empire*. Boston: Houghton Mifflin Company, 1952.

Everett Dick, *Vanguards of the Frontier*. New York: D. Appleton–Century Company, Inc., 1941.

Alpheus H. Favour, *Old Bill Williams*. Chapel Hill: University of North Carolina Press, 1936.

Josiah Gregg, *Commerce of the Prairies*. Philadelphia: J. W. Moore, 1849.

L. R. Hafen and W. J. Ghent, *Broken Hand, the Life Story of Thomas Fitzpatrick*. Denver: The Old West Publishing Co., 1931.

Burton Harris, *John Colter, His Years in the Rockies*. New York: Charles Scribner's Sons, 1952.

Washington Irving, *The Adventures of Captain Bonneville, U.S.A. in the Rocky Mountains and Far West*. New York: G. P. Putnam's Sons, 1850. (Also published by Binfords & Mort, Portland, Oregon, 1954.)

David Lavender, *Bent's Fort*. Garden City: Doubleday & Company, Inc., 1954.

Dale L. Morgan, *Jedediah Smith and the Opening of the West*. Indianapolis: The Bobbs-Merrill Company, Inc., 1953.

Allan Nevins, *Fremont: Pathmarker of the West*. New York: Longmans, Green & Co., Inc. (new edition), 1955.

Francis Parkman, *The California and Oregon Trail*. New York: G. P. Putnam's Sons, 1849. (Also published in various current editions.)

George Frederick Ruxton, *Life in the Far West*. Edinburgh: W. Blackwood and Sons, 1849. (Also published by University of Oklahoma Press, Norman, 1951.)

Edwin L. Sabin, *Kit Carson Days*. New York: The Press of the Pioneers, Inc., 1935.

Maurice S. Sullivan, *Jedediah Smith, Trader and Trail Breaker*. New York: The Press of the Pioneers, Inc., 1936.

Maurice S. Sullivan (Ed.), *The Travels of Jedediah Smith*. Santa Ana, Calif.: The Fine Arts Press, 1934.

Stanley Vestal, *Jim Bridger, Mountain Man*. New York: William Morrow & Company, Inc., 1946.

Stanley Vestal, *Kit Carson, the Happy Warrior of the Old West*. Boston: Houghton Mifflin Company, 1928.

Frances F. Victor, *The River of the West*. Hartford: R. W. Bliss and Co., 1871.

Walter P. Webb, *The Great Plains*. Boston: Ginn & Company, 1931.

Chauncey P. Williams, *Lone Elk, the Story of Bill Williams, Trapper and Guide of the Far West*. Denver: J. Van Male, 1935.

INDEX

FRED REINFELD was born and has always lived in or around New York City. At one time or another in his life he has been an accountant, chessmaster, bookseller, and instructor. Working and playing in chess tournaments has taken him all over the United States. He has written on a wide variety of subjects, including chess, stamp collecting, coin collecting, geology, atomic energy, and the great inventions of the world. Among his books are *Commemorative Stamps of the U.S.A.* and *They Almost Made It.*

From earliest childhood, Mr. Reinfeld was fascinated by American history. When other boys his age were reading stories, he read voluminously in American history. He was particularly interested in western expansion and in the stories of the pioneers, explorers, and trappers of our country. The people he writes about in *Trappers of the West* were familiar figures to him from the time he could read. As he grew older he determined to present a realistic picture of the men who made our westward expansion possible. He feels that many of the books he read as a child were not realistic and *Trappers of the West* was written to fill the need for authentic material on the lives of the mountain men.